CW00591589

BUILDING COMMUNITIES OF THE KINGDOM

This is a really good, theologically hefty, practically grounded book on the mission of the church to be outposts of the reign of God in Jesus. Particularly useful for its contextualizing of the issues for an Australian context. A real gift to the church.

Alan and Debra Hirsch,
Authors, Missional Leaders & Speakers.

Life for many Christians is filled with competing tensions: church or community; worship or practical care; abstract theology or practical engagement; top down or bottom up, etc. In Building Communities of the Kingdom, *Andre Van Eymeren has made a significant contribution that rises above the lines that divide. His vision, (accompanied by careful research) for the coming on Earth of God's Kingdom is holistic, prophetic and possible. Inside this systematic development of what the Kingdom on earth can be are many stories and case studies that encourage the reader that the possible is happening all about us. In the turbulent and unsettling world in which we live, God is up to something generative and creative. This book helps us open our eyes to see and participate in a needed awakening. I commend this book. We need Van Eymeren's voice in both its prophetic and authentic dimensions.*

Dr Andrew Menzies,
Principal, Stirling Theological College

The connection between robust spirituality and best-practice in community development can not be under appreciated. There is always a need for community development practitioners to consider the place of the sacred and of communal spirituality in the development of thriving neighbourhoods. Likewise for Church leaders to connect with their historical praxis in the works of justice and peace over piecemeal and power-plagued charity models. Andre has not only contributed significant study to connecting these ideas, resources and practices but he has also lived it. His is therefore a most worthwhile contribution to this conversation.

Rev. Joanna Hubbard,
Senior Consultant Church Community Development,
Baptist Care South Australia

In this thoughtful book Andre Van Eymeren offers timely reflections from the coal-face of mission in suburban Australia. Drawing upon his significant personal engagement with those facing issues of poverty and social marginalisation, Andre presents a clear challenge to the Australian church to partner with others in seeking that the Kingdom might genuinely come, here on earth as it is in heaven. Tracing both the significant historical shifts that have brought us to this place, and drawing upon perspectives from the disciplines of both theology and community development, Andre is clear that just as the challenges abound so too do the opportunities! It seems God's Spirit is beckoning the 21st century church to engage deeply and compassionately with our local communities, and by leaning into God we can find the love and courage to heed this divine call.

Claire Dawson,
author of *A Climate of Hope: Church & Mission in a Warming World*
(UNOH Publications)

Andre Van Eymeren gives us a thoughtful and hard won treaty here. It is not an outlandish statement to say that if his insights are taken seriously it could revolutionalise the world from the ground up. This book should be especially read by those who suspect so much charity today is unhelpful, but not sure how to proceed with viable alternatives. Andre shares insights and wisdom not simply from his well credentialed research, but also as a practitioner on the front line. These theories are well tested. I hope this book enjoys a wide readership, but more importantly helps people improve their engagement with society and the neighbourhoods they live in.

Dr Ash Barker,
Newbigin School for Urban Leadership (NewbiginHouse.uk)

Faith communities could be the greatest untapped resource in community transformation. Andre thoughtfully explores the vital role churches can play in enabling the small, local actions that make a real difference for people's wellbeing. His challenge is to churches to adopt a holistic approach to community strengthening and makes a theological case for a shift from church communities to community churches. For community development workers in government and other organisations, Andre binds together the role of the church with the access, inclusion and social justice aims so many of us work tirelessly towards. In this way it also serves as a reminder to us all to keep expanding who is involved in building strong local communities and truly make best use of all the assets we have within our reach.

Clifford Eberly,
Community Development Worker, Local Government

Andre Van Eymeren is offering a path of hope at a critical juncture in history! We are beset by extreme individualism, deep fragmentation, and a service-consumer lifestyle. The church must demonstrate a plausible alternative that includes living together as a loving body, developing faithful presence in a particular place, and learning how to share life reciprocally with neighbors instead of ignoring them or trying to fix them. Building Communities of the Kingdom *is the perfect book for church groups and faith communities that want to develop a sound and transformative theology that is matched with practical and liberating pathways for engaging the community. This is parish ecclesiology for the 21st Century. Highly recommended.*

Paul Sparks
Co-Author of the award-winning book *The New Parish*
and Co-founding Director of the Parish Collective

BUILDING COMMUNITIES OF THE KINGDOM

How to work with others
to build great spaces and places

ANDRE VAN EYMEREN

MORNING STAR PUBLISHING

Published in Australia by
Morning Star Publishing
P. O. Box 51
Northcote Vic. 3070
Australia

ISBN 9780995381513

Copyright © Andre Van Eymeren 2016

All rights reserved. Other than for the purposes and subject to the conditions prescribed under the *Copyright Act*, no part of this publication may be reproduced, stored in a retrieval system, or transmitted in any form or by any means, electronic, mechanical, photocopying, recording or otherwise, without the prior permission of the publisher.

Cataloguing-in-Publication entry is available from the National Library of Australia http:/catalogue.nla.gov.au/.

This edition first published in 2017

Typesetting by John Healy
Printed in Australia.

I dedicate this book to Amy and Josh who have travelled with me not only through the writing of this book but all the years and all the experiments that have been its inspiration and insight.

Contents

Introduction

I haven't always found it easy to bridge the worlds of academia and practice. For most of the past 20 years I have been involved in grassroots, coalface mission or community development, in both urban and rural settings around Australia. Working with churches, local councils, social service organizations, schools and the business community, I have been a part of helping communities transform to become spaces that we can call home. On a micro level my family and I have sought to live open lives and build community with numbers of homeless or hurting young people and others, offering a warm bed, welcoming smile and support for their journey.

Over the last few years I have attempted, though not always successfully to move into a more reflective space of which this book is one of the products. I wanted to take time to reflect not only on our mission and community development practice, but broader and perhaps discover an embracing methodology that could allow the church and others to more effectively take up their role as salt and light in the world. There are many working in this space and it is encouraging to see God enabling his people to push forward on a myriad of new paradigms for engagement with His world. I hope and trust that this book can be a helpful addition to what is already being done.

Our starting point for this journey is a vision of shalom portrayed by the prophet Isaiah (65:17-25). He longs for a world where communities regularly come together to celebrate and remember the good things in their midst, where stories are shared and there is laughter and hope for the future. The hallmarks of these communities are acceptance, a sense of belonging, but, deeper, a sense of a shared reality and future that opens the door for each to find their place. Unfortunately one of the hallmarks of our communities tends to be isolation and disconnection. Young people are often labelled as the problem, the elderly ignored and undervalued, anyone who is different tends to be shunned, particularly the marginalized experiencing homelessness, mental health issues, dislocation and an incredible sense of a loss of self. The community Isaiah sees is one of reconciled relationships, active involvement, genuine connection, people having not only a place to live but a place to belong and flourish.

I had the privilege of attending a two-day workshop in Melbourne, which was asking the question how do we go beyond the safe city? Melbourne is seen as being a safe city by international standards, but how do we go beyond that to create a city where people can flourish, growing to who they were meant to be and living their purpose out of that sense of being? I was heartened to hear many references to values that I saw congruent with my understanding of Scripture. I soon realized I was with people who may not acknowledge the root of these values but who you could consider people of peace, influential in their networks and open to partnerships for the greater good of the city. Over the time I've been involved in community development I have come across many such people and have often found them easy to engage with, full of vision and energy for new and better ways of doing community, and often more receptive than the church to pursuing these avenues.

I'm pleased to say the tide is beginning to turn. However, I have been concerned at the malaise of the church around matters of engagement at all levels of society and the equipping of the saints for works of service wherever they find themselves. In many ways the church has shown itself to be a good provider of welfare and other services. It is a well-known fact that the majority of welfare in Australia is in someway linked to the church, and for many these have become necessary and vital services. In addition the church is often opening its buildings for a range of community activities that when working well provide opportunities for those outside the church to build relationships with believers and for the church experience to be de-mystified. However, if we want to effectively work towards Isaiah's picture of Shalom there are some fundamental paradigm shifts that need to be understood and enacted.

These new understandings relate to a paradigm of God's Kingdom that allows for the people of God to have a robust engagement with the world. Looking at our churches, one could be forgiven for thinking that God's concerns revolve around salvation and building the numerical numbers of the church. Whilst salvation and the fellowship of the believers are important to God, our preoccupation with these things points to a misunderstanding of God's final intentions for the world and indeed his present activity in it. There are many biblical pictures such as Isaiah 65 that point to God's intention to bless the city or the community. He even encourages the exiles in Babylon to work for the prosperity of their new city.

If it's true that God cares about cities and indeed the whole of life and we are called to be salt and light within this broader picture, what shape does church need to be to most effectively engage with those around it? Shape here refers more to internal postures and attitudes of a gathered group of people than what happens on a Sunday morning. The shape then naturally affects this expression. The focus then shifts from the gathered community to the scattered people of God. Jesus says in John 13 that they will know you by the love you have for each other. If this is true it begs two questions - first, do we genuinely love each other? Second, if we do genuinely love each other, how do people get to see that love, to feel it, so it becomes tangible for them? How do we live corporate Christianity in spaces where individuality seems to reign, as is often the case in the workplace?

With workplaces and the broader community in view it is a natural jump to explore the culture we find ourselves in and its roots. The activities of the church do not happen in a vacuum; we are part of a very complicated web of historical, scientific and cultural change. With the rise of rationalism and the breakdown of the village, industrialization and the eventual collapse of Christendom our societies have evolved quite dramatically. With the commodification of technology and the dizzying pace at which it develops we can find ourselves awash in a sea of consumerism quickly losing sight of the shore of purpose and meaning, living in a hyperreal world where symbol is just as, if not more, important than actual reality.

We see the natural effects of the breakdown of the village even today. In local communities and broader, fractured relationships lead the way to dysfunctional societies where in extreme cases people die in their houses and are not discovered and, we presume, not missed for many, many months. This is also reflected in the suicide epidemic, particularly evident amongst teenagers. In the closing chapters of this book we will explore ways that the church can work with others to recreate that sense of village, to be part of restoring the relational web of support that we all need. This book draws heavily on the work I did for my Masters' thesis of the same name, but is hopefully more readable and interesting. I have not referenced all these connections as it would be too laborious, however I believe I have been true to my original sources and so open the possibility for further reading.

My hope in writing this book is to show the links between God's Kingdom, the role of the church and the place of community development as a valid part of the church's missiological response to the world. I also hope it will be instrumental in the forming of partnerships with people of peace towards the common good.

Chapter 1. - Setting the Scene: A Snapshot of Australian Society

Addressing poverty and inequality is important from a health perspective. However, contrary to the prevailing social-determinants (and social-justice) orthodoxy, the core social challenge is not primarily a poverty of the means to the end of 'the good life' as it is currently defined and pursued; it is a poverty of the end itself.

Richard Eckersley

In the vision statement of the organization I used to work with we recognized there are two realities within Australian society, the one you see and experience depends on where you sit and how you orientate your attitude. A research technique known as Appreciative Inquiry (AI) looks at what already exists in a community, organization or individual. It seeks to recognize and celebrate the strengths, exploring ways to build on those strengths. It involves time with individuals, exploration of their narrative and aspirations, then looks to draw together common themes and priorities. The process itself can often be redemptive and helps individuals and communities recapture who they are.

I worked with a local council in Melbourne where they decided to take a strengths based approach to planning and asked me to facilitate four workshops that sought to uncover hidden potential that the community possessed, with a view to creating a vision of what their community could look like in four years. So the elements of strength and aspiration were highlighted and the participants encouraged to explore their own strengths, as well as their local connections and what they could bring to the planning table. After which the focus turned wider with the participants naming strengths and potential contributions they saw in the organizations and institutions around them. The result was astounding, hearing stories of one community group that raised $900,000, another who successfully engaged with disengaged young people from their ethnic community, re-introducing them to school and family. Others included a temple community that regularly feeds thousands of people. Aspirations included a greener community, more local jobs and neighborhoods that actively welcomed newcomers. As the night drew on, the energy and buzz in the room was palpable; people began to see that they could make a difference in their community. Many of us have probably been involved in nights similar to this, however I suspect a key difference is that the energy was generated from within the group, they weren't responding to a presentation, they were responding to their own ideas.

Setting the Tone of Our Conversation

Fiona Cram points to a 4-D AI cycle of Discovery, Dream, Design and Destiny, in which through initial inquiry, dreaming about what could be, designing a future and taking action, transformational change is sourced from the community itself.[1] The people we have in our heart to help, become the very vehicles for change to happen. From the outset we need to hold a high view of the community, in fact to see the community through God's eyes and with him and them seek to move latent skill to action and stymied potential or aspiration to fulfilment. We will unpack the AI methodology later in the book, however it is useful to say here that AI has been criticized for taking an overly positive approach and turning a blind eye to negative and difficult experiences. AI practitioners comment that this isn't the case. AI is in fact a starting point rather than a naïve and idealistic endpoint.[2] Whitney and Trosten-Bloom also point out that individuals and groups tend to move towards what they study, which leads to the obvious conclusion that we want people to become more aware of the positives.[3]

Disempowered Contributions

The alternative is a needs or deficit look at the world, which focuses on the short falls, the negatives and what is missing within communities, organizations and individuals. Both are views of reality, yet the outcomes of the methods of exploration are vastly different. The first easily lends itself to the empowerment of individuals and whole communities, the second is a key building block of our welfare system and tends to take responsibility for change away from the individual or community, ultimately leaving them disempowered.

Steve, who became a friend while my family and I were involved in a missional community in Pakenham, an outer South Eastern suburb of Melbourne, was a victim of the welfare cycle. An alcoholic, drug user and

---

1.   Fiona Cram, "Appreciative Inquiry," *MAI Review* 3 (2010).
2.   Michael as cited in Cram, "Appreciative Inquiry."
3.   Whitney and Trosten-Bloom as cited in Cram, "Appreciative Inquiry."

petty criminal, Steve had spent the majority of his adult life in and out of prison. Because of his health, substance issues and prison history he found it hard to get productive work and generally move forward with his life. When he came across Big House Communities he was living in the shed of a known paedophile. For all intents and purposes this was an isolated man in crisis; he was on government benefits and would have been for many years. Yet as we got to know him we discovered a man with incredible ability to make things and despite all his life experiences, someone with a soft heart, who just wanted to help others. As people took the time to get to know him and hear his heart, he began to blossom.

I remember one extremely hot day, Amy was out at the shops with our son and one of his friends and the keys got locked in the car. She rang me but I was tied up and couldn't help, so I rang Steve. Within minutes he appeared in the car park, shirtless and on his bike, there to help. And in no time he had opened the car and retrieved the keys. When I caught up with him about it he was beaming as I thanked him and told him the difference his help had made.

Living was never simple for Steve and eventually his alcoholism cost him his life. However, he was a man that others looked at and thought needed welfare, needed the help of others, but perhaps what he really needed was more chances to help others.

I live on a public housing estate in Melbourne's inner north with four housing towers, each with twenty floors. The towers are filled with people who are receivers of welfare. From new arrivals to single mums, the elderly and some who have been living in the towers for over forty years, now living alone after raising their family. Many suffer with poor mental and physical health as well as various addictions. When we think of welfare in this context it can be seen as a good and necessary thing. Secure housing has been provided, income support is readily available, as well as regular meals run by churches and other support agencies. In addition, when there are special needs, particularly around medical issues, special services can be put in place. Whilst at times welfare of this sort might be necessary, the overwhelming message given to the community is one of passivity. In a sense the combined services are saying, 'all you're capable of is sitting back and receiving everything we want to give to you, but you better comply.' There is very little exploration of people's skills, abilities, perspectives and, most importantly, aspirations. The delivery of welfare has become a substitute for the building of relationship and the uncovering of potential.

Indigenous Australia

When it comes to disempowering and not uncovering potential, Australia has a poor report card with Indigenous Australians. As our country was settled Captain James Cook declared it terra nullius - land belonging to no one. Aboriginal people were seen as not having a strong attachment to the land, particularly because they didn't farm it and so no treaty was formed with them. Instead they were put under the protection of British law. Hear the word 'protection'! However this was somewhat haphazard. John Hirst in his book *Looking For Australia,* explains that the early governors were told to ensure that the Aboriginal people were not harmed but that of course taking their land and introducing thousands of foreigners to the land hurt them. Despite having the protection of British law it was very rare that a white man would be brought before a court or punished for killing Aboriginal people. Governors themselves sometimes led expeditions against them and there were ruthless killings over land as white people began to dominate the country.[4] The history of the relationship between Aboriginal and white Australia has always been problematic and it continues today. In many places there is a call to stop welfare to Aboriginal communities and a recognition that they must have jobs and their children be well educated.[5] I fear even in this latest attempt at integration, the strengths of Indigenous Australia have not been seen or valued.

As evidence of this, at the time of writing there are protests being held around the country about the forced closure of Indigenous communities in remote Western Australia. This is a complex issue, perhaps beyond the scope of our conversation, however the point remains that Indigenous Australia has not been recognized as the gift it is to the broader Australian community.

The glass is half full

Australia as a country and as a people has many gifts to offer. If we are to look at Australian society through the glass-half-full lens we would recognize the fact that we live in a relatively safe democracy where we have

---

4.   John Hirst, *Looking For Australia* (Melbourne: Black Inc, 2010), 46.

5.   Hirst, *Looking For Australia*, 49.

the opportunity to be involved in the political process at a number of levels. Apart from voting for political representatives at the local, state and federal level, we have the opportunity to input into planning and the shaping of policy. However this means we have to be active and prepared for some hard creative work.

I was asked by an outer city council to facilitate a series of community workshops. Unlike many similar events these workshops were aimed at collaboration and empowerment. The International Association of Public Participation has a spectrum, which outlines the continuum of relationship between a government body and a community.[6] According to this spectrum collaboration is about partnering with the public in decision-making, including the development of alternatives. These conversations then become incorporated into a council's decision-making process to the maximum extent. Empowerment is understood as putting the final decision into the hands of the public. Once made, the council would then implement the decision.

This council wanted to take things a little further and explore the community's perception of its strengths. These strengths would be evident in individuals present on the night, their relationships, the organizations in their community and the bigger institutions such as schools, hospitals and so on. The groups were asked to imagine the type of community they would like to see in four years. Using this frame they began to map the strengths. One community group has been able to raise over $900,000 just by keeping people informed on social media about the progress of the campaign. People with cooking skills, religious temples with massive catering capability, cycling clubs, sporting communities, facilities, aspirations such as community gardens, social entrepreneurialism as a way to engage and train young people were all unearthed.

Being active in this way helps us to see that influence is not as far away as we might think. The genuineness at which the council is approaching these conversations is astounding. They are committed to a sustainable community-led approach to development. It is harder to connect with people of influence at the state and federal level, yet not impossible if we are

---

6. "Public Participation," *IAP2 Resources*, accessed 15 March, 2016, https://www.iap2.org.au/resources/public-participation-spectrum.

prepared to be proactive. Those who show up tend to be ones influencing decisions.

If we are looking at Australia through a glass-half-full lens we might also acknowledge our ability to pull together in a crisis. These stories are reflected to us by the media coverage of natural disasters such as the Black Saturday fires and the Queensland floods. There was plenty of evidence of country and city communities alike pulling together to not only preserve life but to rebuild communities. Will Ockenden, a rural reporter with the ABC tells a firsthand story of the devastation of the 2011 Toowoomba flood and touches on the amazing rebuilding effort that happened faster than anyone could imagine.[7] The resilience and community spirit of the Queensland people was remarkable with over 200,000 people affected by the floods across the state. Brisbane saw massive clean-up teams, managed by the defence forces but including 55,000 registered volunteers, with many thousands more just turning up in the muddy streets with gumboots and shovels.[8]

Australian Geographic online editor, Carolyn Barry was personally affected by the floods and the devastation left in their wake. First hand she saw the layer of mud and destruction as she gathered with family at her great-uncle and aunt's house to begin the massive clean-up. In the floods the house was covered in water to about a metre from the gutters. Inside was a layer of mud that covered everything. All the big furniture items were turned upside down or found on their side, with the stench of mud and rotten food almost too much to bear. As the family surveyed the damage, confused about where to start, Eddie from Cleveland walked in and asked if he could help. Then another couple of women came and before they knew it there were a dozen people helping clear the house. In addition others dropped by with BBQ food and much needed cold drinks. It was summer in Brisbane

---

7.   "Toowoomba: Queensland floods one year on," *ABC News*, last modified 9 January, 2012, accessed 15 March, 2016, http://www.abc.net.au/news/2012-01-09/toowoomba-queensland-floods-one-year-on/3761292.

8.   Lindsay Murdoch and Megan Neil, "Salvation comes with brooms and gumboots," *Sydney Morning Herald*, 16 January 2011, http://www.smh.com.au/environment/weather/salvation-comes-with-brooms-and-gumboots-20110115-19rv6.html.

after all.[9] Because of the Aussie Spirit of getting in and lending a hand, what would have taken days was completed in just a few hours.

If we take a positive look at our country, for the most part we enjoy a high level of prosperity and believe generally that we are better off than past generations. It was recognized internationally that the stimulus package put in place as the Global Financial Crisis hit genuinely kept our economy buoyant as other world economies spiraled out of control. I'm writing this looking over Melbourne's Docklands from my vantage point inside the library, which I enjoy for free. It's a sunny autumn day and many will be out in the parks, which are beautifully maintained by our local councils. Others will be hitting the beaches and the countless restaurants, all in perfect safety, enjoying what the world's most livable city has to offer. These sorts of simple everyday pleasures will be repeated around the country. The majority of people in our country are employed and have warm houses to go home to with plenty of food to enjoy and people to connect with.

For all my friends who work, as I have, with others encountering a different reality on a daily basis, I realize this is an idealized view of our country, yet one that is a lived experience for many and the result of living in a country for all intents and purposes still reasonably remote from the rest of the world. I believe we are so aware of the issues around us we are almost at saturation and need a balancing perspective to remind us that all is not bad. I am not immune to the alternative reality endured, but in fact believe there is incredible potential present in that gloomier world. Here I want to point out that ours is a country that has many obvious signs of the presence of God's Kingdom. We see this in the natural beauty around us, in the relative peace that we enjoy and in the examples I've shared above. God's Kingdom is of course present in the murk, but it is not as obvious and a positive look at its presence I believe will help us see the green shoots in the concrete, in those places where we may not normally be aware of its presence.

So if you'll continue to indulge me a little further there are more positives to reveal. In our supermarkets of all shapes and sizes you will mostly find what you are looking for. The shelves are stocked and the quality of the food is generally very high. Though costs are rising most food remains affordable. We've all seen the pictures on the news of people in the developing world,

---

9.   Carolyn Barry, "Personal perspective: inside the flood clean up," *Australian Geographic*, 15   January   2011,   http://www.australiangeographic.com.au/blogs/ag-blog/2011/01/personal-perspectives-inside-the-flood-clean-up/.

trying to shop for goods in supermarkets with empty shelves and lately the number of humanitarian crises are increasing where people in refugee camps or disaster zones are waiting for their allotment of food.

Australia has public health care with a Medicare system that for the most part is accessible and of a high quality. I had a recent stint in hospital and found the public system for the most part to be efficient and caring. Despite long waiting times, once you are actually in the hospital or in a clinic the level of care is high. I have been impressed that three doctors I am connected with have been talking with each other outside of my appointments to ascertain the best course of treatment. For me it has all been free.

We have an education system that is free at the point of delivery. For the majority of our married life Amy and I have had young people living with us, most of them have struggled with school and have not felt they belong or that it is relevant for them. Of course there are serious issues that we need to look at including how to structure alternate learning environments. However there are more and more experiments taking place and more young people finding a process of education that works for them. The school my son attends is a good example of flexibility, where it supports students in individual learning plans and is open to alternatives outside of school. There is no uniform and teachers are referred to by their first name, better cementing relationships with students. Chris, a former Salvation Army Captain, now works as a youth worker for a Catholic school in an environment set up for teenage kids who don't fit into the traditional system. He sees the alternate school as offering a place to belong, where young people can learn in an environment that is friendly and focuses more on how to live well in our world.

There are many debates around whether the multicultural experiment that is Australia has worked. However it seems for the most part it has. We reap the benefits of people living in our country from a wide variety of backgrounds. I walk up my busy inner Melbourne street of a night to see the Thai, Chinese, Vietnamese, Italian, Baha'i, Afghani and African restaurants opening for business. Filtered in amongst these eating establishments are burger joints and pizza shops, as well as a few different expressions of 'The Local.' Australia as a nation has welcomed people from other nations. We now have a rich and diverse culture evidenced in our art, varying perspectives in public debate, businesses with high work ethics and commitments to creative problem solving. As well as many places to enjoy the unique contribution of different beliefs and worldviews.

Despite recent issues around asylum seekers and scaremongering about the Muslim community, the majority of Australians are welcoming and embracing of multiculturalism. In the lead up to the first Welcome Party Campaign in June 2011, Adelaide pastor Brad Chilcott gathered a dozen representatives of organizations working in the refugee space. His vision was to recruit Australians to create a culture of welcome. The group has grown to six centres around Australia all working to provide opportunities for individuals, families, businesses and other organizations to promote what has become some core Australian values of diversity, compassion, generosity and the commitment to giving all people a fair go. With others the group has been active in lobbying for change in Australia's asylum seeker policies. They believe the best way to bring change is to facilitate opportunities for genuine relationships to form where stories, aspirations and hopes are shared.[10]

Mariam Veiszadeh was born in Kabul, Afghanistan, during the Soviet war of 1984. Due to the war her family had to flee Afghanistan in 1988. Over the next three years Mariam and her family would travel to the Czech Republic, Germany, India and finally Australia. After being enrolled in school in both Germany and India and experiencing the pain of making friends and then having to create a completely new start, Mariam arrived in Australia. She was shy. Not speaking any English, she was immediately enrolled in English as a Second Language (ESL). Mariam says she is grateful for the educational opportunities and for allowing her and her family to call Australia home. She sees that multiculturalism is here to stay and its expression goes deeper than dumplings and kebabs. Her call is for us all to work together to ensure that the Australia we call home doesn't just tolerate diversity, but celebrates it.[11]

Our land's natural beauty, Indigenous Australians and the rich heritage we have because of them, as well the immigrants with whom we share our country and the vast array of skills, perspectives and food that they bring with them, really makes us the lucky country. Our access to top quality

---

10. "About," Welcome to Australia, accessed 21 May, 2016, http://www.welcometoaustralia. org.au/about.

11. http://www.welcometoaustralia.org.au/stories/item/367-mariam-veiszadeh

education and health services means we can for the most part chose to live well. Perhaps overall we are at our best in a crisis where we demonstrate selfless care for the other.

The murky truth

Appreciative Inquiry is not immune to the deficits or the faults in individuals, communities or societies, it simply chooses as a starting point to see the strengths, and from this base helps communities appreciate what they have to tackle the issues. Because we are not sitting in a room together, workshopping the strengths and solutions evident in the Australian community, I need to outline some of the issues. I want to paint some real concerns that are present in our country and that can tend to be passed over either because of a lack of awareness or a propensity to put our head in the sand, a posture which, if not explicitly, is implicitly reinforced by an entertainment-soaked, 24/7 news cycle driven media.

During 2012 I was part of developing a significant body of research on the social environment for young people and the rising epidemic of youth suicide.[12] The research was based in Melbourne and Sydney yet the findings relevant to much of Australia. We looked at the societal drivers of media, the arts, business, education and politics, asking members of each driver how the driver had contributed to a negative social environment particularly for young people and how the driver could be restorative. Then in Melbourne we ran a series of three conversations called Hope Talks on the topic of youth suicide. The first was a media lunch with a journalist who was exploring the phenomenon and opening up the issues of suicide clusters. In the South East of Melbourne there was a cluster with the tag line of *13 by 13*. That thirteen young people had pledged together to take their lives by the end of 2013.

Around these young people was a pervading sense of hopelessness that things in this life would not get any better. They believed the myth that they would be together, able to party in the next life. They were dealing with the grief from others in their friendship group taking their lives, as well as a lack of understanding and a lack of connection with significant adults. They had not been helped to see a story or a vision beyond their immediate

---

12. "Project 217: The Social Environment and Young People In Australia Today," Biblevic, last updated February, 2013, accessed 20 November, 2015, http://biblevic.files.wordpress.com/2012/01/project-217-report1.pdf.

circumstances. Many were struggling at school and were succumbing to the negative messages around the importance of achievement according to the system and what underachievement says about who you are. All these factors put together led to the tragically sad belief that after death, they would connect with old friends, and be in better circumstances. Their parting words to each other being *see you on the other side.*

A school chaplain, after the death of a student's parent, wanted to make sure that the group of young people he was caring for had a way of processing grief. He knew that it was important for each young person to have someone they could talk to, someone they trusted who could help them process what was happening around them. As he investigated this with the students who were all boys, he discovered that none of them had that significant adult in their lives.

The Social Environment for Young People

Exploring the social environment for young people is like a litmus test or the canary in the mine for a society. If young people are generally doing well, experiencing stability, connection, growing to maturity, finding their place and purpose they will be fairly resilient to the ups and downs in their lives and the community around them. If these things go missing, for young people their rudder is gone, the guiding light has been turned off, which is indicative of a potential crisis in the broader community. Statistics from the Australian Bureau of Statistics show that each year, 9 out of 100,000 young men aged between 15 and 19 will end their own lives. 3 out of 100,000 young women in the same age bracket. This increases to 19 and 5 respectively at the 20-24 age bracket.[13] These figures perhaps don't tell the whole story as they don't generally include ways of death such as single car accidents and so on. For Indigenous young people the story is even more grim, with the Northern Territory Youth Suicide rate sitting at 30 in 100,000 with the Kimberley rising to 80 in 100,000.[14]

---

13. "1370.0 Measure of Australia's Progress, 2010," ABS, last updated 15 September, 2010, accessed 21 May, 2016, http://www.abs.gov.au/ausstats/abs@.nsf/Lookup/by%20 Subject/1370.0~2010~Chapter~Suicide%20(4.5.4).

14. Gerry Georgatos, "Australia's Aboriginal children – The World's Highest Suicide Rate," *The Stringer*, 3 August, 2013, accessed 21 May, 2016, http://thestringer.com.au/australias-aboriginal-children-the-worlds-highest-suicide-rate/#.Uc0x1pXmpvc.

Our work over 2012 showed some core elements going missing in the social environment for young people. These included a sense of identity, significant relationships with trusted adults, a lack of enduring values, a missing overarching meta-story, which leads to a diminishing sense of purpose, a diminishing sense of village and a lack of coherence in society generally.

Relational poverty was seen as a major contributing factor to a negative social environment for young people. We discovered it was common for young people to report feelings of isolation, alienation, fragmentation, anonymity and feeling dehumanized. I'm generally a fan of local media and have used it on many occasions to highlight good news stories within local communities. However when it comes to young people local media tends to fall in line with the sensationalist agenda of many mainstream media outlets. Young people are often portrayed as community problems with giant pictures of graffiti or vandalism splashed across prominent pages of the paper. On the flip side much has improved in the way of policing young people, but even here there continues to be a lack of understanding on the part of the police between appropriate risk-taking behaviour that young people engage in and behaviour that crosses the line into being anti-social or dangerous. Although again good work is being done in the court system regarding young people, there is still a general lack of understanding of what life is like for many and the powerful effect of programs like restorative justice, which is a very relational approach to help young people understand the impact of their crime on the victim. It also helps welcome the offender back into society. The media, police and justice system tend to increase the level of alienation young people experience, rather than working together to create a more inclusive environment. The predominant motif is to punish wrongdoing over rehabilitation and reducing recidivism.

The story continues, and remember we are using young people as a reflection of society more generally, particularly the vulnerable in society. So for young people, feeling excluded from community makes it difficult for them to form a positive identity and a sense of personal worth. If they are disconnected, who will help young people navigate through the many voices that they are bombarded with on a daily basis? These voices include all forms of advertising, the internet, messages evident in music, movies, through the media, parents, teachers and their own peer networks. Other factors which affect young people include the drive to be successful, which can come from the family unit, school and many other places, and the negative messages received when they don't measure up.

A number of years ago my family and I were involved in teenage foster care. Jane (names are changed to protect privacy) came into our home after a number of broken placements. She was disengaged from school and was connected with a pretty unhelpful crowd. Working with our agency the task was to provide a stable environment for her to continue at school. Jane was not a fan of school and struggled with the discipline and routine necessary to succeed. She believed she was dumb and to an extent unable to learn. As carers my wife and I were dismayed (not surprised) by the way she was treated at the school. Amy became a firm advocate for a more tolerant approach, one that saw and valued her as a person. Jane very quickly found herself in trouble, many times for quite minor things. She felt rejected and unwanted at school, the message being made ever clearer by some at senior leadership level. Instead of being able to adapt a learning approach to suit her, the school tried to make her fit the box. She eventually dropped out.

Of course the other side of the equation is the arguments of the one versus the many, needing to maintain order and discipline, and the exasperation of trying to cope with and cater for different learning styles. This points to the need for systemic reform, starting with the very DNA or building blocks of the system. Through this particular example we can see the general need which is highlighted by educational researcher Sir Ken Robinson. In a short summary of his thinking available on YouTube, he outlines the state of current education, that essentially we are educating people using a system designed in the Enlightenment, i.e. for students to become units of production rather than for human flourishing.[15] Schools can be like factories - bell times, subjects taught in silos and students taught in batches according to age. Robinson sees that education is driven by an economic model as well as by certain presuppositions about who can learn and how they learn. Who is smart and who isn't. Education tends to be about standardization, he believes we need to go in the opposite direction, towards divergent thinking, a core capacity for creativity.

So a little test: how many uses can you think of for a paperclip? An average person may come up with 10-15, someone who is really good at it could

15. Ken Robinson, "Changing Education Paradigms," *YouTube, RSA Animate,* last updated 14 October, 2010, accessed 15 November, 2015, http://www.youtube.com/watch?v=zDZFcDGpL4U.

come up with 200 because they say why can't the paperclip be say 100 times bigger than a normal paper clip and made of foam rubber. This question was given to 1500 kindergarten children, 98% of them scored at genius level for divergent thinking. The same children were tested 5 years later at ages 8-10, only 50% scored at genius level. They were tested again another 5 years later, with a smaller percent coming out at genius level. The research showed that we all have the capacity for divergent thinking and that it diminishes as we get older. A key factor for young people as they get older is that they get educated. They are told there is one answer - it's at the back of the book but don't look. They are told that copying is wrong as opposed to learning how to collaborate, which according to Robinson is essential for personal and societal growth. So overall he sees that the culture of our educational institutions needs to change.

I'm focusing so much on education as it is a core part of young people's experience and through this an essential shaping agent of our society. I've had the privilege of witnessing two attempts to change the model of education. One was happening over 15 years ago in the Northern Suburbs of Adelaide, a community experiencing systemic poverty and generational unemployment. The principal of the high school where I was a chaplain saw much of what was being described by Robinson and initiated a learning annex where young people who weren't fitting into the system could be nurtured in other ways including working in a number of social businesses that the annex created. The space also provided accommodation and a listening ear for many of the students that worked there during the day. I remember being so impressed by the dedication and care of the staff as well as the general engagement of the students.

A more recent example I was closer to was based in rural Tasmania in a town owned by a youth and community organization Amy and I were working with. The village was set up to care for disaffected young people. They would come into the village and begin their stay with a host family, of which we were one. They would then be given the opportunity to complete schooling or take on a vocational education program based on their interest and connected to one of the businesses in the village. For example they could work in the motel learning hospitality, or in the gardens learning horticulture and similar for basic mechanics or metal work. In the context of a community that cared for and loved them they got to experience real work and the feeling of success.

In both these examples there were many ups and downs and much learning along the way but they illustrate a way of creating worth and meaning and a recognition of individuality and are very congruent with a method of community development known as Asset Based Community Development (ABCD) that we will be exploring later in the book.

A Conversation About Values

Values are another area where the social environment for young people has been damaged. Our postmodern era tends to promote a plethora of self-seeking values that can be summarized, 'as long as it feels good and doesn't hurt anyone else, then its ok.' These values leave young people (and others) rudderless and impressionable to a range of influences, where the loudest voice tends to win.

A few years ago in Australia there was talk of a values-free education. Many of us scratched our heads, wondering how anything can be free of values. Each one of us brings our biases, which come from our upbringing and continue to be shaped by our experiences, including our experience of faith or non-faith. The problem manifests when we don't acknowledge those biases and act and speak as though we have the sole window on the truth. Recently there has been a strong push within Melbourne to remove religious education from schools. Unfortunately, some people of faith have become defensive about this and have been shown to be inflexible. Much of the response has come from a fear base, that the next generation of children won't have the opportunity to hear the gospel at school. This type of fear response fails to understand the place of the Bible and the Christian faith in the creation of the very schools that want to remove religious education. If people of faith were able to own this truth, we could seek to uphold a value system congruent with the gospel and create other spaces where more overt sharing would be appropriate.

As an outside observer Indian Christian academic Vishal Mangalwadi is uniquely placed to highlight the importance of the Bible in the formation of Western culture. In the introduction to *The Book That Made Your World* he sees that great literature, art, science, liberating technology, genuine heroism and nation-building, and great social institutions were all inspired by the Creator's vision of what reality is all about, as seen through the pages of the Bible.[16] Therefore as we think about Religious Education in schools we can do so with great confidence, however our approach and what we teach may need to change. This change needs to include a palatable way to inspire young people with life giving values that move away from selfishness to the embrace and service of the other.

However, in our society there is a lack of an underlying values system that can provide young people with a coherent path to the future. In a later chapter we will explore the journey to postmodernism which will illustrate how value systems have become individualized and largely created around what will benefit the individual rather than values for the common good. At the outset this way of doing values can make sense, however at a deeper level it has been one of the factors that has led to the decay of a sense of community, with all its associated problems. As a sense of community has dissipated so has the concept of the village. The old adage it takes a village to raise a child is still relevant, however, sadly, rarely practiced. It's the idea of the extended family and the neighbourhood being involved together in the raising of children. When Amy and I were running an op shop in the outer south eastern suburbs of Melbourne as part of the missional community we led, we had the honour of being visited regularly by an African family. Whenever they would come into the shop the children would run round the end of the counter looking for 'Aunty'. In their culture every woman of a certain age was aunty and every man, uncle. Each took responsibility for the raising of the children. In our culture we have the opposite where we have put so much pressure on the nuclear family, which I'm not convinced is the biblical model of family, that many crack under the pressure of trying to raise children for a civil society, pay the bills, keep food on the table and just juggle the incredible busyness of everyday life.

If what we value has pushed us to individualism, then the family and the community has certainly been the victim. In the early days of our work in the outer South East of Melbourne I was part of a consultation with local council on the needs of our fast growing local community. As part of the consultation we were broken up into table groups and asked in various ways what we thought were the key needs of the area. The core issue that every table came back with was loneliness and isolation and this was particularly being seen in the new housing estates. Due to, amongst other things, the

---

16.   Vishal Mangalwadi, *The Book That Made Your World* (Grand Rapids, MI: Thomas Nelson, 2016), xxi.

long work hours that many spent away from the community, sometimes as far as 60km, many people didn't know their neighbours. If partners with young children were left at home they often had no transport to go out and mix with others. Added to this, because of large mortgages and other bills, if a financial need arose or a partner lost their job, then the precarious house of cards that was often the financial norm very quickly crumbled and people ended up at the local food bank driving their new car, which they couldn't afford to stop paying.

Related to this notion of a lack of an underlying or guiding values system and a village that has gone missing is a rejection of any kind of meta-narrative or big story. This is a story or cultural myth (not an untruth but what we tell ourselves about our culture) that helps us to make sense of the world around us and helps us to answer the 'why am I here?' and 'what am I made for?' type questions. The ability to invest in this story allows one to move above and beyond the small world we tend to create for ourselves and allows us to appreciate and work towards the common good.

Ultimately the story that has gone missing from our culture is God's story of creation, forgiveness and renewed life which opens the door for the Kingdom of Heaven to be present in the world now, inviting us in the present into an eternal reality. With this as the overarching meta-narrative it is possible for each culture to live in its own iteration of the story. As a culture is adopted into this story it allows for communities, families and individuals to find their place under its rich canopy.

However, the reality in Australia today is that this story has been rendered invalid or irrelevant. Filling the void has been a plethora of alternate stories around consumerism, hyperreality where symbols are more important than product and the immediacy of the internet and social media all predominantly with an individualized, hedonistic intent. Instead of a coherent story young people are faced with a whirlwind of options which often leaves them overwhelmed, bewildered, confused, addicted, lonely, directionless and open to abuses of all sorts.

Cyberbullying is an example of what can happen in this space. In the good old days (not sure they were that good) when I was growing up, if you were bullied, which I was, then when you went home it had stopped, it was over, you could breathe and prepare, with perhaps some anxiety, for the next day. Young people today find it very difficult to turn off their phones and the internet (as do many adults) and so the abuse can continue 24/7 and have much more permanent effects, i.e. on websites and Facebook, and deeper psychological effects where anxiety over what is being said to and about them can increase at an alarming rate, and if not dealt with can turn into a neurotic psychosis. Young people can often then resort to self-harm to ease the internal pain, the ultimate result of which is suicide. Of course this isn't the only road to self-harm and suicidal behaviour.

Richard Eckersley, director of Australia21 and researcher into youth health and wellbeing, wrote an article for Crikey on this phenomenon in 2012.[17] In it he criticizes the media, health and education professions for focusing too much on the individual as they think about youth mental health, for looking at self-harm and suicidal behaviour as an individual illness requiring treatment. Eckersley states that even if social explanations are offered they tend to focus on structural changes in the family, education and job prospects, conflict, exclusion and disadvantage. They fail to address questions of what makes life worth living for young people. Eckersley cites Theo Padnos, an American prison teacher, who sees youth violence as an attempt to intervene against a nothingness in a world stripped of meaning and self-identity. In this context, Padnos argues that young people can even see violence as morally grounded. Eckersley includes self-violence in this and reinterprets self-harm as a reflection of a deeply human need to turn intangible suffering into tangible pain, which turns the passive experience into something that can be controlled.

As mentioned earlier, due to the rise of individualism and a host of other factors including social media, young people have lost the anchor afforded them through a cultural understanding of their importance and connection. Australian novelist Ruth Park puts it like this, "Whatever hardship came our way was all on the outside. Inside we knew without doubt, that Life was aware of us and somehow had us in its care." Disconnection has left many young people stuck in their heads, vulnerable to a materialist culture and struggling with the associated raft of emotions.

Eckersley is also concerned about our culture's focus on the external trappings of the good life which increases the pressures on young people and others to meet unrealistic and inappropriate expectations, which in turn heighten

---

17. Richard Eckersley, "The Denial Behind Youth Suicide," *Crikey*, September 14, 2012, http://www.crikey.com.au/2012/09/14/the-denial-behind-youth-suicide/.

the risk of failure and disappointment. Young people's identity then tends to be fashioned from their personal attributes, achievements, possessions and lifestyles, lessening the positive effect of shared cultural traditions and beliefs. Young people and others then miss the most important step to wellbeing, the quality of relationships with each other and the world.

Eckersley points to a raft of other factors that play a part in youth health problems like change in diet, sleep, physical activity, experience of nature, drugs, sex and relationships and at a social level broader changes in the worlds of family, education, work, religion, leisure and entertainment, natural environment and an uncertain global future. All these things are determined by our modern western culture, our collective worldview of values, beliefs and priorities. Eckersley is essentially pointing to the existential crisis that is affecting young people and the broader society at large.

An antidote (at least in part) is for us to begin to embrace the full extent of the meta-narrative laid out for us in the Scriptures. Currently there is a lack of leaders who embrace this meta-narrative in all spheres of society. Research shows that young people are looking to individuals for guidance and perspective, because their interpersonal relationships are often lacking effective role-models, they turn to celebrities and sporting stars. Listening to what they say and watching how they act, taking their cues as to what's important from them. Unfortunately many of these leaders do not have strong value-based compasses themselves, some even shy away from this type of notoriety. Yet because of the voracious need of young people for heroes to look up to, they are followed anyway, sometimes with disastrous consequences.

What I have sought to do through this brief look at culture through the eyes of young people is to show that we are not in Kansas anymore. In terms of the cultural perspective of the church, which is steeped in Christendom and often in our country expressed through a 1950s worldview, we are definitely in a brave new world. The cultural maps that we have developed for ourselves largely do not relate to the current climate. We need to do the hard hermeneutical work of reinterpreting God's word for the world we find ourselves in now, and let that understanding guide our practices both internally as the church gathered and externally as the people of God in the world.

A Response to Where We Find Ourselves

A guiding question to help in this journey: what is good news to this city, this community, the world we live in? From my balcony I can see a corner of the city, but directly in front of me as I look out is a public housing tower. There are in fact four towers each with about twenty floors with numerous flats on each floor. The estate comprises a bewildering mix of race, age, abilities and life circumstances. The kids love to play on the oval, the basketball court and of course at the after school care program run by dedicated volunteers that takes place every day. It's not uncommon for us to open our balcony door and hear their chatter and play and even their disagreements, which at times can be very vocal. Many of the children, along with their parents, are refugees from Africa, looking for a better life in Australia. Quite often when my wife and I take our little dog out to the oval some of the children will come up and want to play with him. They are the brave ones, as many have been taught to fear dogs, coming from their village contexts of dogs equaling disease. The towers also contain many elderly people, some of whom like to walk the grounds each morning, doing their stretches and various exercises. Some walk stiff legged and it is unclear how old they are, but I suspect many are in their late 80s or 90s, migrants from another era and place, living out their days strong in the sense of community around them.

Others have lived in the flats almost since they were built, raised their families and seen them move onto other things. Now they live alone or with a partner in a big flat that I'm sure at times feels empty, even with the memories of family, fun and laughter. Finally, there are people living with various challenges including being single parents, addicts, alcoholics, those who suffer from various mental and physical health challenges, those caring for others who are sick and those suffering from the various effects of entrenched poverty.

Ours is a very vocal community and again with the balcony door open sometimes you can get more than you bargained for. It's wonderful to hear the laughter and play of the kids, however sometimes the conversations echoing from the street are not as life giving, loud arguments that can escalate very quickly, drunk people walking home from the pubs and clubs and even the odd loud sneeze of a morning. The conversations that disturb me the most involve only one person, often loud and perhaps even focused on something or someone who is not present. There are many volatile people in our neighbourhood who may appear rational and even kind, but live on a knife-edge of anger and frustration with only a hair trigger separating calm from rage.

Out the front of our building there are places to sit and quite often there are a mix of people some connecting, others living more of a solitary life. There is a lady who spends the whole day sitting and crocheting. She displays her work and sits there, often with her feet up and smoking, interacting with the ones who want to buy from her.

The day we received the key for our apartment, I remember the three of us walking up Brunswick Street with about seven musical instruments between us. I had expected heads to turn and us to be seen as some spectacle, but no one batted an eyelid and thus began a journey of discovering the diversity of our new neighbourhood. As well as all the struggle and hardship our community is one of incredible creativity. Many walls in the area are covered with brightly painted designs depicting cartoon characters, indie scenes, political commentary and a host of different patterns. Much of the work has been done by local artists. It's also quite common to walk down our street of an evening and hear music floating down from the jazz club or see a busker or two strumming away or tapping out a rhythm on the drums.

The area where I live has a past reputation for organized crime, however many have transcended that reputation, particularly as the community has gentrified, with old townhouses being renovated and factories being converted to comfortable modern living. While most aren't connected to a criminal element there remains a very activist culture, with most of the street posts littered with posters for rallies, Marxist conferences and marches. I'm not sure the point he is trying to make, but there is also a man who regularly walks down the street holding a giant papier-mâché carrot.

So this is my community, in part where I am placed to be salt and light. A core question for me is, what is good news for this diverse and divergent community?

Jesus very clearly says that he is the good news, so what does it mean to take Jesus into this neighbourhood and more generally into the places and spaces we all occupy? As Christians, and especially for Evangelicals, our default is to think that means we have to evangelize wherever we go. That being the hands and feet of Jesus means verbally announcing the gospel message wherever we find ourselves. Whilst to some extent admirable, this thinking can lead to rather extreme actions. There is a man who regularly stands on a corner in the central business district and literally yells the gospel or at least announces it very loudly to people passing by. He tends to focus on the effect of sin and the need to be saved from all its implications. Whilst however poorly he is proclaiming a part truth, it stands in stark contrast to the rest of what is happening in the city. His manner is abrasive and his approach does not engender relationship with him or portray a loving Father who desires a relationship with people.

A focus purely on evangelism can lead to missing what is really going on in people's lives. A former youth worker tells the story of a university student who was part of a Christian group on campus. The group became aware of 'The Four Spiritual Laws', essentially the gospel story told in a way that creates a pathway to salvation. The student, in his zeal and equipped with his new tool hit the campus, going up to fellow students and inviting people to follow Jesus. He went up to one particular student who attempted to relay something back to him, but he kept ploughing forward with his task. Finally the receiving student was able to communicate that someone close to him had just died. The first student had totally missed the cues and was set on the task of communicating his message and through this failed to show any empathy or open the door for genuine relationship. A focus purely on evangelism can lead us to disingenuous relationships, where we only befriend others so we can say that they have been saved, which provides us with another notch on our belt.

In many parts of the church the main concern is personal salvation and naturally this colours any interaction with the world. Taken to its extreme this thinking sets up an unhelpful dualism that allows us to distance ourselves from this world and any responsibility to work for the common good of those around us. I often ask my students about their soteriology (how salvation works) and eschatology (how God's going to wrap up this phase of eternity), saying that our understanding of these two things show us what we think is important to God. Naturally this flows to what we are prepared to put our energy into.

I'm pushing the extreme and of course personal salvation is a part of God's plan, but it is only a part. There is so much more to what he is doing in the world, so many more hallmarks of his work. As a church our myopic focus on salvation has left us for all intents and purposes voiceless. We have excluded ourselves from many debates where our voice is desperately needed. In Australia there are not many in senior church leadership or in the church generally who have seriously engaged with the plethora of ethical issues that modern life throws at us. There are pockets of Christian ethicists looking at our use of money, the effects of the explosion of technology, the role of media, how far science should go in the use of stem cells etc., the effects of global warming and others exploring issues of food security, homelessness and generational poverty to name a few issues, but for the most part the church is quiet in the public debate towards the common good. Where we do seem to have a voice is around a particular set of moral issues to do with sexuality and right to life. Whilst these are important issues to debate, our propensity to talk at length about these things has left a bad taste in the mouths of many Australians, and again has shown us not to be counter-cultural, but culturally irrelevant.

Sadly we tend to miss in part a potential remedy to this situation. Generally the church, whilst good at caring for people, preaching and teaching on biblical truths and a host of other things, misses an important opportunity by largely not equipping its people to recognize what God is doing in their neighbourhoods, at work, in their sporting clubs and so on. What flows then is a reluctance to see work as ministry, and the worker as minister. The subtle or perhaps not so subtle message is that the real ministry happens within the bounds of the gathered Christian community.

The good news is that the Kingdom of God is so much broader than the church. God's activity in the world is not limited to our institutional expression of Church and in fact encompasses the whole globe, with our responsibility being to recognize his hand and at times lack of his hand and join him in his enterprise.

Reflection Questions

1. As you think about your country, city, community or neighbourhood what thoughts and feelings come to mind?

2. How could you apply Appreciative Inquiry to your mission / ministry?

3. How do conditions for young people in your community, shed

light on how the vulnerable are faring?

4. How do your values affect your engagement or otherwise with those around you?

Chapter 2. - God's Dream for Our Cities and Communities

This, as we have seen, is what the resurrection and ascension of Jesus, and the gift of the Spirit, are all about. They are not designed to take us away from the earth, but to make us agents of the transformation of this earth, anticipating the day when, as we are promised, 'the earth shall be full of the knowledge of the Lord, as the waters cover the sea.'

Tom Wright

I was tempted to call this chapter the sealed section, as I'm conscious that not everyone reading this book has a Christian faith. However, I wanted to explain where my community development practice is rooted and by that show where and how I believe the Christian faith can participate, with others meaningfully in the dialogue around how to build a better world.

The Biblical language around God's agenda or dream for the world is not altogether helpful for our modern idiom. Despite being a constitutional monarchy the word kingdom is foreign to us and at best conjures up images of colonialism, unfettered autocracy, unhelpful controls and general irrelevancy. At worst it speaks to us of corruption, adultery and despotic rulers. None of which are helpful in our understanding of what it means for God's Kingdom to be present with us and God's agenda to be worked out in our midst.

The Kingdom or the rule of God is a central theme throughout Scripture and is a symbolic way of talking about a tangible progressive experience of a transformed world. Traditionally Evangelical Christians (my tradition) have believed that the expression of the Kingdom of God is primarily through the reformed life of the believer, in which the Holy Spirit now dwells. We have understood the Kingdom therefore to be an inner reality with, for some, very little outward expression in terms of societal transformation. This leads to the belief that when we die we will go to Heaven, the place where God's rule is complete.[1] The extrapolation of this understanding has left very little room for many evangelicals to engage meaningfully in any social reform or even want to be connected into contemporary debates apart from ones focused on personal moral issues.

---

1. Tom Wright, *Surprised by Hope* (London: SPCK, 2007), 24.

Thankfully there are other voices from within the Church and Evangelical Christianity who advocate for a broader understanding of what God is doing in the world and how he invites all of us to join with him. These voices echo the cries for justice, purposeful community, prosperous city living, inclusion and freedom, particularly for the poor and marginalized, evident in passages such as Micah 6, Isaiah 61, 65, Luke 4. The nature of the Kingdom of God therefore is intrinsically linked with who God is and his purposes for creation. John's gospel or telling of the life of Jesus sets this in a cosmic frame, recognizing that all things were created through Christ. This sets the history of the nations and nature itself within a larger framework, that of God's plan and purpose, which has its source in God's love for his son Jesus and through him his love for all his creation.[2] John goes on to say that the one through whom all was created is now present or accessible. This sets up the context for the good news that the reign of God over all things is at hand.

For those who have had a bad experience with church or otherwise or, like Nick Cave, don't believe in an interventionist God, these ideas can be unpalatable or even repulsive. For me they are the basis for the world that we are all working towards. The prophet Isaiah believed that a time was coming: when everyone in a community would be seen and valued for who they are; disease and death would be minimized; people's basic needs would be met; and there would be the opportunity for all to find meaning and purpose. These things would be the effect of Shalom or God's reign.

As I digest this list of outcomes, I see the goals of many local government departments and social service organizations being ticked. These biblical concepts are congruent with contemporary understandings of human flourishing and for the church that embraces them; they can provide a robust rationale for partnership with other agencies. God's purpose in creating the world was to provide a way for him to spend time with his creation, including of course humankind. In this light the Kingdom or the reign of God is not an escape for redeemed souls, as many who adhere to traditional understandings of salvation believe, but is the action of God bringing history to its fulfilment. This is seen in a renewed earthly humanity marked by peace, happiness, prosperity and wise and just government (Ps 82, 144, Isa 1:1-9).

---

2.   Lesslie Newbigin, *The Open Secret: An Introduction to the Theology of Mission*, (Grand Rapids, MI: Eerdmans, 1978), 30-31.

Unfortunately the orthodox protestant view of the Kingdom of God only being present in the heart of the believer has set up a dualism between this world and the next or, as Jurgen Moltmann puts it, the Kingdoms of nature and grace.[3] N.T. Wright builds on this understanding that many protestants see the work of the Kingdom through the lens of a false understanding of eschatology, namely, that they will go to Heaven when they die. This makes Heaven a static place rather than the dynamic all-encompassing benevolent rule of God. This understanding relegates the work of the church to the saving of souls for the future. Whilst a personal relationship with God is an exciting part of God's Kingdom being present in the world, our preoccupation with this aspect has affected the church's ability to contribute meaningfully to the creation of a better world. We have been preoccupied with only one aspect of the whole story.

Wright argues instead for us to see the Kingdom in terms of God's promised new heaven and new earth, a promise that we can all participate in as we partner with God in his work of restoration, to a full life for all pre-death. However things are not as rosy as this picture may hope to paint. Because of sin (essentially our desire to go our own way) Creation continues to try and shut itself off from God's future. The result is the negative picture of our society painted in the first chapter. The world we experience, where individualism is king, commercialism fuels the economy, infotainment gives us our perspective on the world and government tends to be short sighted and reactive. Despite these negative traits God's positive future is kept open to us primarily because of the work Jesus did on the cross. By dying and through his resurrection he paved a path of obedience and set a model of the way life could be. He was an advocate for the poor, a radical feminist, a wise teacher, painted a picture of a world where all are equal, demonstrated a balanced life where time focused on the spiritual was as important if not more than other aspects of our being. Most importantly his death opened the door for the forgiveness of humanity's desire to go our own way and with that forgiveness the possibility of a new and brighter future, which continues to be held out to each generation.

---

3. Jurgen Moltmann, The *Trinity and the Kingdom: The Doctrine of God*, (London: SCM, 1981), 208.

The Design and Purpose of God's Kingdom

The possibility of a brighter future is sustained by the selfless work of God. To better understand this we need to briefly explore a doctrine that came into existence post-Bible (or post the establishment of the canon). The word 'trinity' is not mentioned in the Bible, yet it can be drawn together thematically through the various references to God throughout the breadth of Scripture. It is a way of describing the three-ness and one-ness of God. The Father, the Son (Jesus) and the Holy Spirit are three separate beings, yet they are one. To the best of our understanding they exist in perfect community. Imagine a relationship where each of the participants are in perfect sync with each other, unity if you like. They each have a particular role or function, yet carry out their tasks in love for the others and in humble submission to each other. In one of his many teaching conversations with his disciples Jesus talks about preferring to serve than be served (Luke 22:27). In this way the Trinity or Godhead becomes a model for all human community and acts as a guide to the establishment of a healthy, flourishing society.

Father God – The Creator

Each member of the Trinity has a distinct function. The Father is the creator. In Genesis (first book of the Bible) we see The Father bringing order out of chaos. Light and dark are separated, the boundaries of water and land are established and then all living things are created. Traditionally it is understood that this creation happened in six literal days and on the seventh God rested. This understanding has at times pitted Evangelical Christianity against science. People who ardently argue for this view forget that the style of the creation account we find in the Bible is similar to other creation accounts found in various ancient near east literature. If we were to categorize this literature we would see them as creation myths, similar to stories from Indigenous Australians' Dreamtime. The Genesis account therefore is not necessarily trying to tell us exactly what happened, but more set principles in place. For example, God brought order out of chaos, through the creation of the world we see around us. I'm more concerned with that picture than arguing about how exactly it happened, seven literal days or theistic (God centred) evolution and so on. The other principle that comes out of the creation story is that humankind was given a mandate to look after all of creation. I think we can agree that collectively we have neglected this mandate.

The current state of the natural world around us is cause for concern. Climate change scientists continue to alert us to the affect of rising levels of the sea due to increasing temperatures that are melting the polar ice caps. This continues to threaten small island nations, even in our own region. According to the latest European Environment Agency Report whilst there are improvements in pollution levels, we are still suffering the effects of a mismanaged environment.[4] The report states that Europe's natural capital is not yet being protected, conserved and enhanced, in line with previously stated ambitions. Whilst air and water quality has improved, loss of soil functions, land degradation and climate change remain major concerns. In Europe 60% of protected species and 77% of habitat types are in an unfavourable conservation status, leaving the continent vulnerable to loss of biodiversity. Health risks including air and noise pollution continue to rise, particularly in urban areas where population is increasing. In 2011 there were 430,000 premature deaths in the EU attributed to fine particle matter and 10,000 attributed to environmental noise leading to coronary heart disease and strokes. The growing use of chemicals has also been cause of increasing endocrine diseases and disorders.

There are sounds of hope, change is coming, use of fossil fuels is down, however the dismantling of unhelpful systems of production will take some time, particularly where people's livelihoods are involved. David Cash, Dean of the John W. McCormack Graduate School of Policy and Global Studies at the University of Massachusetts, Boston, is hopeful, as nearly two hundred national governments have committed to make cuts to greenhouse gas emissions.[5] The challenge will fall to us who occupy and work within cities, states and provinces. Cash points out that the 2015 Paris climate summit was strikingly different to its predecessors in that what he calls the subnational governments were engaged. These 'non-party' actors held many side meetings, where they made their own public commitments. They were embedded into the official adoption of the Paris Agreement as it

---

4. "Executive Summary," European Environment Agency, Synthesis Report, accessed 9 January, 2016, http://www.eea.europa.eu/soer-2015/synthesis/report/0c-executivesummary.
5. David Cash, "The Paris Agreement: The First Local Environmental Pact," *The Conversation,* 8 January, 2016, accessed 9 January, 2016, https://theconversation.com/the-paris-agreement-the-first-local-global-environmental-pact-52483.

sought to keep average temperature increase well below the global tipping point of two degrees above pre-industrial levels, preferring the increase to be no more than one and half degrees.

The following was part of the pre-amble to the Paris agreement:

> Agreeing to uphold and promote regional and international cooperation in order to mobilize stronger and more ambitious climate action by all parties and non-party stakeholders, including civil society, the private sector, financial institutions, cities and other subnational authorities, local communities and indigenous people...[6]

Encouragingly, this is to be done taking into account everyone's human rights:

> Acknowledging that climate change is a common concern of humankind, Parties should, when taking action to address climate change, respect, promote and consider their respective obligations on human rights, the right to health, the rights of indigenous peoples, local communities, migrants, children, persons with disabilities and people in vulnerable situations and the right to development, as well as gender equality, empowerment of women and intergenerational equity ...[7]

Because of the previous vacuum of international action on climate change, cities, states and provinces have become increasingly proactive in developing policy. There have been experiments with carbon taxes, rebates, cap-and-trade programs, building codes, private-public partnerships, innovation incubators, university-government partnerships and streamlined permitting for renewable energy projects.[8] All these initiatives are in essence a reclaiming of the original mandate given to human kind by God to care for his creation.

This care needs to be lived out in meta-multi national policy as well as in daily action. Waste is a big issue in the building I live in. We have a room where everyone brings their household garbage. There are two types of bin, one goes to landfill and the other is for recycling. In 2014 I was part of a small project aimed at helping people in the building take more care

---

6. "Adoption of the Paris Agreement," United Nations, Framework Convention on Climate Change, last updated 12 December, 2015, accessed 9 January, 2016, http://unfccc.int/resource/docs/2015/cop21/eng/l09r01.pdf.

7. "Adoption of the Paris Agreement."

8. Cash, "The Paris Agreement: The First Local Environmental Pact."

in dividing their rubbish. A small group gathered to talk about waste and the importance of recycling, we then creatively represented what we had been talking about. Everyone in the building received a copy of what we had created. Due to a number of managerial issues the project wasn't as successful as it could have been, however if apartment buildings all over the city were to implement similar strategies to help their residents become aware of issues like recycling, there would be a significant impact on the landfill of the city. These sorts of results help us as individuals realize that we can make an impact and encourage sub-national entities to keep pursuing greener paths towards the future.

Jesus the Liberator

The next member of the Trinity is Jesus or God's son who is known as the liberator. Traditional Evangelical Christianity has interpreted this as Jesus being the individual's liberator from sin. Whilst Jesus does play this role, the liberation he brings is broader and deeper. Jesus was born into a nation that was a vassal state of Rome, they were captive economically and emotionally, a common occurrence throughout Israel's history. Many of the people were farmers and despite working the land, barely had enough after taxes to meet demand, and no resources to build a more prosperous future for themselves or their community. There was also a religious vacuum. Previous to John the Baptist, appearing a few months before Jesus' public ministry commenced, there had been no prophetic activity for four hundred years. Into this fairly desperate situation came Jesus a revolutionary, proclaiming good news to the poor, freedom for the captive, sight for the blind, freedom for those who suffer and that God's favour was with his people (Luke 4:18-21).

Ched Myers picks up on these themes in his commentary on Mark's gospel. He sees that Jesus was a non-violent revolutionary.[9] Focusing on context, Myers helps us to understand that we interpret the gospels from where we sit. For example, the movement he is a part of now, *The Radical* (meaning back to roots) *Discipleship* movement, has its origins with the Indochina war and the U.S. civil rights movement. Christians on the left side of the political divide were moved to a just disillusionment with government and other shapers of society. This disillusionment pushed some back to their roots and a more revolutionary, justice-orientated understanding of the

---

9.   Ched Myers, *Binding the Strongman: A Political Reading of Mark's Story of Jesus* (Maryknoll, NY: Orbis Books, 1988), 7.

Gospels. Lutherans looked to Bonhoeffer, a pastor, author and teacher from Nazi Germany who spoke out against Hitler's regime and was martyred. Baptists looked to the Anabaptists, who wanted to take the reformation further than Luther and his contemporaries had in the early 1500s, aiming for a church outside of the influence of the State.[10] Methodists looked to the work of Wesley, responsible for changing much of the culture of working class England through establishing small groups or class meetings focused on helping people follow the teachings of Christ with a focus on showing love, good works and holiness.

Whilst the Radical Discipleship Movement saw Jesus as a revolutionary, how did the original hearers of Jesus' teaching and the writings of the gospel respond to these themes? The people of Jesus' day, as we experience today had a mixed response to his message. Some were amazed at his authority and others thought he was blaspheming against God and deserved to die. Still others, namely the religious leaders wanted to kill him because he threatened their power base. Many of his followers were convinced that he would deliver Jerusalem from their captors in some kind of revolutionary overthrow of the current power structures. Jesus was more interested though in setting an environment where people could thrive and flourish no matter what was happening around them. If this involved a change in religious or political structures so be it, however revolution of this sort wasn't his starting point.

Jesus and Personal Transformation

Jesus' teaching on and action towards liberation started with people's internal attitudes. Warning: the following few paragraphs are confronting! It was Ghandi who said, 'be the change you wish to see in the world.' Ghandi was a fan of Jesus' teaching and in fact much of his own teaching was based on it, particularly a passage from Matthew's gospel know as The Sermon on the Mount (Matt 5-7). A core part of this teaching is known as the beatitudes and they are a key to personal and societal transformation. Dietrich Bonhoeffer writes a short commentary highlighting their radical nature.[11]

---

10. "1525 The Anabaptist Movement Begins," *Christianity Today,* accessed 10 January, 2016, http://www.christianitytoday.com/ch/1990/issue28/2838.html.

11. Dietrich Bonhoeffer, *The Cost of Discipleship* (New York, NY: Touchstone, 1959), 105.

To set the scene, Jesus is on a mountain outside the city, crowds of people have followed him because word has got around that he is a healer and someone who teaches with different authority to other religious leaders. Jesus has already called a small band of loyal followers to be his disciples. He is addressing them, with the crowd looking and listening over their shoulder.

Blessed are the poor in spirit, for theirs is the Kingdom of Heaven says Jesus.

The disciples have just given up everything to follow him. He called them from family businesses, lucrative earnings and a host of other environments. They obeyed the call and were following Jesus' promise of a better way, a bright future as part of the Kingdom of Heaven. These words would have hit hard as they remembered they had no security, no possessions and not even a patch of dirt to call their own. They didn't even have any spiritual experience or special knowledge to draw upon. They were poor and inexperienced yet prepared to put their hope in Jesus who called them.[12]

This concept of sacrifice speaks to our motivation. Why are we invested in social transformation? What is the reason for our commitment? If the answer is something to do with us: monetary reward; kudos; status; to feel good about ourselves; to fulfil our desire to be needed; or even to please those we look up to we are involved for the wrong reasons. Jesus says the Kingdom of Heaven or a transformed world is for those who will leave everything, even reputation for him and his agenda. Some reading this will not believe that a life following a God they don't believe in is worthwhile, and since I am not trying to change your beliefs, I would encourage you to reflect on what it means to serve those around you altruistically. A hospital is built for the sick not the doctors, a school for the students, not the teachers, and so for community work, for the community we serve, not us the workers.

The idea of altruistic practice or sacrifice is an aspect of the concept of human flourishing. It's been defined as an "ongoing self-actualization that promotes the personal and interpersonal good."[13] This understanding provides a clear link to humanistic psychology, and Maslow's hierarchy of needs. More recently this has been expressed as 'self-determination

---

12. Bonhoeffer, *Cost of Discipleship*, 107-108.

13. Maureen Miner and Martin Dowson and Stuart Devinish, *Beyond Wellbeing: Spirituality and Human Flourishing*, (USA: Information Age, 2012), 8.

theory.' Proponents propose that when basic human needs like autonomy, competence and relatedness are met, individuals can experience wellbeing, vitality, growth and inner harmony.[14] Humanistic Psychology, like the biblical narrative, asserts that human beings are basically good and need the opportunity to grow and express this inner reality.

Whilst not complete, Humanistic Psychology is perhaps the strongest pointer to Miner and Dowson's understanding that flourishing has both an inner and outer component. The inner is characterized by actualization, which is non-contingent on circumstances, enables a sense of self and agency, and allows a dynamic equilibrium or integration of personal experience. Outwardly, flourishing takes root in altruistic behaviours, which flow from a harmonious self-expression, integrity in line with one's true self, and productivity in activities that benefit the self and others.[15]

Whether you seek to become poor in spirit or self-actualized, as the psychologists would say, the result is the same, your life becomes open to the service of others, for their benefit.

Blessed are they that mourn, for they shall be comforted.

For the follower of Jesus, the call is to clearly see the state of the world, with all its hardships, trials, guilt and suffering, and in addition not buy into what the world sees as success. Henri Nouwen reminds us that to follow in the footsteps of Jesus is to open our hearts to the trials going on around us. In our modern media-soaked world it is all too easy to become desensitized to yet another humanitarian crisis, not to mention the one suffering on our doorstep. The remedy for this is to mourn, to be bearers of sorrow, to let ourselves feel the pain of others and the world, which can then lead us into hoping for a better world. For those of faith this better world is the growing presence of the Kingdom of God and in fact our task is to work for this coming, partially now and to be completed in the future when Jesus brings heaven (his full presence) to earth.[16]

Again this may not be the motivation you are looking for, however if we are to work together towards a better world, we need to grow our ability to empathize with those who are suffering. Our professionalism often teaches us to distance ourselves from our 'clients,' giving us a range of self-protective

---

14. Miner and Dowson and Devenish, *Beyond Wellbeing*, 13-14.

15. Miner and Dowson and Devenish, *Beyond Wellbeing*, 15.

16. Bonhoeffer, *Cost of Discipleship*, 108-109

activities to put into practice. When we distance ourselves from the other in this way we de-humanize them, giving them the role of someone to be pitied and helped. We needn't fear opening ourselves to the pain of the other if we are able to keep a clear vision of the way the world could be and the part we are to play. This helps us to hope in a bigger picture rather than becoming overwhelmed in the struggles of an individual.

Blessed are the meek: for they shall inherit the earth.

Meekness is often associated with powerlessness, yet Jesus gives a series of anecdotes where he encourages those experiencing oppression to turn the tables on their oppressors, though not in the way you might expect. He paints a scenario all too common to the Jewish farmer or peasant worker of his day. He sets up a context of someone seeking revenge for wrongdoing. Instead of encouraging an eye for an eye or a tooth for a tooth, Jesus says when someone hits you, let them hit you again, if someone is suing you, give them more than what they are asking for. If an occupying soldier asks you to carry his pack for one kilometre, carry it for two. In these simple acts the powerless becomes powerful because they choose to serve or be generous. This is so counter-cultural to our individualist rights-based existence as to almost sound offensive, yet it was this kind of meekness that enabled Jesus to repair our broken relationship with God and set a model of social interaction into play. The promise is that as we let go of our rights and stop trying to possess things and people and stop trying to manipulate situations to meet the needs of our ego, as followers of Jesus we will be with him and enjoy the fruits of a renewed, perfected earth, which will have a society hallmarked by the characteristics we all long for - justice, peace, prosperity and hope.

I struggle to write this next paragraph, because it points to the role of the Church, which sadly has fallen short of its place in the world. The Church, the people of God, the followers of Jesus are meant to be a foretaste of this society. So if anyone were to walk into their company they would begin to experience this type of world. Unfortunately in our country the Church is not known by these characteristics. If you were to ask the average Aussie what their view of the Church is you would get responses like 'irrelevant to my life,' 'don't accept how the message is taught,' 'out-dated,' 'don't trust the clergy,' 'don't believe in what they teach,' or 'just too busy to think about it.' You could probably add others from your own interactions. Interestingly social research group McCrindle found that 43% of people (not including regular attenders) feel the Church is beneficial for them and 88% feel it is beneficial for their community. Yet somehow this doesn't equate with them actually attending church on a regular basis (at least once a month).[17]

The same infographic displays the perceived needs of the respondents' communities. The highest priorities were parklands and walking tracks and teen activities and youth groups. The local church and religious services were placed much lower on the list of priorities. This shows a couple of things: first, that Australians see the Church and religion outside of the rest of society (although this depends on the way the categories were established in the original piece of research) and that the role the Church could have, with others in meeting the needs of the community, is missed. On a list of personal priorities with family relationships as the top priority followed by physical and emotional health, finances, career, social connection, the spiritual and religious side of life rates the lowest priority for Aussies. Yet for the most part we are satisfied with this low level of individual spirituality.

Despite these statistics, the point and the call to meekness remains true. The media, feeding off the Church's persona, often portray the Church as other worldly, disconnected, with an air of arrogance. The Church tends to come across the same whether the media are portraying an Easter service, a response to clergy abuse claims, or advocating to not change the legislation around marriage or abortion. The Church seems to have forgotten the need to be meek, not scraping for a place in society or seeking to justify itself, but rather living out the call to meekness, a radical counter-cultural life, that focuses on serving the other, regardless of reputation and position.

Serving the other regardless of reputation and position is the connecting point for those that don't share the Christian faith. Even in community work where we talk about meeting the needs of the other, our motivations can still be ego driven, as we manoeuvre for recognition, promotion or even simply to feel valued. Subtly our focus can change from good intentions to help others, to the meeting of our own needs. The antidote is humility, a right assessment of ourselves and a recognition 'that we are only two or three bad decisions from ending up in the same position as those we are attempting to help.' According to Matt Maudlin, CEO of Servants Community Housing,

17. McCrindle Research, "Church Attendance in Australia," *The McCrindle Blog*, last updated March 2013, accessed 10 January, 2016, http://blog.mccrindle.com.au/the-mccrindle-blog/church_attendance_in_australia_infographic.

the road to homelessness can be very quick and has the potential to affect anyone. Another friend of mine discovered this firsthand. Pete was a very successful building contractor, based in Melbourne. He thought nothing of flying to Brisbane for lunch and then home again. He ran a business with a lot of people working for him and lived a life with all the trappings of success. In a matter of weeks, due to some bad business decisions, he watched his business crumble around him and found himself living under a bridge in country Victoria.

Blessed are they that hunger and thirst after righteousness: for they shall be filled.

I wonder how you would answer if someone were to ask you, what is your deepest desire? Would your first thought be for something material or something about a particular person or a way you would like a relationship to be? Or the desire could be something deeper such as peace in your life. These few words about hungering and thirsting after righteousness encourage us to desire at a whole other level. They focus on something that could be seen as other-worldly, yet is already present with us. The idea of righteousness points us, according to Bonhoeffer, to a personal and earthly renewal.[18]

For me, the past couple of years have been a renewal of sorts as I have pressed pause on an activism that left me exhausted and emotionally, physically and spiritually worn out. I got to a point where I desired more than a stressed, harried existence that felt like running from one fire to the next. Through the guidance of a spiritual director I realized amongst other things my longing for a feeling of safety and stability. In a sense, the knowledge of a more constant awareness of God's presence around me. As I grew in this awareness (and I'm still growing) I became more conscious of what the bible calls sin, things in my life that actually caused a block in my relationships or a hampering of my own actualization. As awareness dawns I then have a choice whether to actively deal with those inconsistencies or continue to let them shape my existence.

Jesus did not succumb to sin in the same way that we do, however on the cross he still experienced a void in his relationship with his father which caused him to cry out in utter loneliness and desperation. The longing for renewal does not stop with the personal. As we looked at in the last chapter

---

18. Bonhoeffer, *The Cost of Discipleship*, 110-111.

the world is also in need of renewal. Young people are committing suicide, homelessness is increasing, the earth is warming and already some small island nations are experiencing the consequences of our excesses and the list could go on. Righteousness in this context is the desire for God to come and set things right, not a temporary fix, but a permanent solution. In other words, that the world and human society would be managed in the way it was created to be.

So for us as people who care about the spaces and places we occupy and the people who occupy them with us, what is the picture that we hold of the way the world could be? When push comes to shove how much do we desire it and what would we be prepared to give up to see it become a reality?

Blessed are the merciful, for they shall obtain mercy.

The concept of mercy is linked to empathy. Colloquially this has been described as 'walking a mile in another's moccasins.' Our world tends to be big on sympathy, with responses to tragedies that often put the carer in the same emotional space as the one being cared for. It's exhausting to be trying to explain how you feel to someone only to have them respond something like, 'I know exactly how you feel,' and then proceed to tell you about an experience they perceive as similar. The difficulty here is that even if you have experienced exactly the same event as someone else, because of your different emotional world and past experiences, your feelings will probably be quite different to the other person's. Sympathy tends to hamper the other's ability to share their world. Empathy or mercy on the other hand is the task of putting our own emotional world on hold and truly entering the space of the other with a desire to help them understand their own experience.

Mercy is also linked with identification. Jesus identified with us by leaving the comfort of the relational Godhead and incarnating or coming into the neighbourhood. He identified with us to the point of dying so that we could have a relationship with God. This understanding of mercy propels the follower of Jesus into a life of love and connection with "the downtrodden, the sick, the wretched, the wronged, the outcast and all who are tortured with anxiety."[19] Bonhoeffer goes on to say that no distress is too great, no sin too appalling for the follower of Jesus because they have already been

---

19. Bonhoeffer, *Cost of Discipleship*, 111.

shown mercy. So often in my country the Church wants to hold itself apart from the suffering of the world, just in case its purity is affected by a drug addict or a homeless person caught in the grips of poverty. It claims a righteousness that is akin to that of the Pharisees in Jesus' day, based on a removed religiosity. Instead Jesus' call with these words is to remember that we are part of a fallen creation having been shown mercy, a mercy which compels us to in turn show mercy to others.

A key to showing mercy or empathy is to give the gift of ourselves to another. The best way we can do that is to be fully present with them. A former boss and mentor of mine had perfected the ability to give this gift to others. He was CEO of a large youth and community organization and many would have seen him as a workaholic. However if you were with him for a one-on-one meeting you knew by his eye contact, his lack of distraction, attentive body language, his ability to help you explore your world, and his lack of interruption or probing questions that his only concern during that meeting was you. Over the years I have worked to give this gift to others but have only falteringly succeeded. It's a skill that can be learnt and one that is essential if we are truly going to identify with those we seek to empower.

Blessed are the pure in heart: for they shall see God.

Unless we are part of a specific industry that uses purification processes or relies on purified products, the concept of purity tends to be foreign. It may even have negative connotations of a naïve innocence or even prudishness. Here Jesus is referring to those who have surrendered their will or volition to him, in order that his way becomes their way.[20] This sort of purity brings with it a childlike simplicity, allowing us to be captured by the beauty that surrounds us and intrigued by the people we meet. It also saves us from the duplicity of divided desires as our only true want is to work in partnership with God for the world he created. It allows us the space to come to rest and contemplate the mystery that is God, the source of our being and any of our action in the world. We are then freed to truly see God.

Blessed are the peacemakers: for they shall be called the children of God.

I admire my friends who are prepared to put their body on the line for what they believe. *Love Makes a Way* is a movement of clergy and other Christian leaders who occupy the offices of politicians with the simple call to release all children from Australian immigration detention centres. They

---

20. Bonhoeffer, *Cost of Discipleship*, 112.

43

simply move into the waiting area of the office and pray and sometimes sing. They present this simple demand to the politician or their staff. Quite often they are able to sit in the offices for most of the day eventually being removed by the police. They have found much support from the police and the courts, with none of them having a conviction recorded.

Other more radical friends believe in non-violence and peace to such an extent that they are prepared to disrupt war games. Every two years in Northern Queensland the army and navy come together to train and participate in real-to-life, but simulated war. Four young activists snuck onto the base where the games were being played and started playing their own games such as Frisbee and football, some of the soldiers even joining in. This activity by civilians brought the whole games to a temporary pause. Every year other non-violence proponents barricade the road bridge to Swan Island, a military base that houses Australia's most elite soldiers.

Non-violence is a hard won practice and if we are to take it seriously it requires much self-examination and relates to more than whether we are physically aggressive. Elsewhere in the gospels, Jesus equates being angry with someone to murdering them, the emphasis here is that in each case the relationship is broken and so it is as if the other is dead. Currently in Australia there is a growing awareness of the depth of domestic violence. Programs are being put in place to help those affected, however unless the inner violence of the perpetrator is dealt with the violence will continue. Jesus calls his followers to possess peace, that internally we embody a trust and assurance that God is in control of all things, including our lives. From this basis we are able to offer peace to others and bring peace to circumstances that would normally be riddled with violence. Of course we can't control whether the other is violent or not and we may need to be prepared to suffer for our peacemaking.[21]

A deeper aspect to this process is the letting go of our need to be right or justified in our actions. It involves a relinquishing of the terrible need to always explain ourselves. This will enable us to face others and difficult circumstances with a calm confidence built on the internal knowledge of a loving God who is ultimately in control. As we embrace these truths and practices we will partner with Jesus and in this way become sons and daughters of God.

---

21. Bonhoeffer, *Cost of Discipleship*, 113.

Of course non-violence and peacemaking is not only the domain of the Christian faith. Ghandi and many others have paid the price for refusing to take up arms. There are countless relationships where people of all descriptions have sort the ways of non-violence and conflict resolution. Whether coming from a Christian perspective or not, being able to bring peace into troubled families and communities requires a high level of self-awareness and an understanding of where the source of our peace comes from.

Blessed are they that have been persecuted for righteousness' sake: for theirs is the kingdom of heaven.

The last of the beatitudes refers to those that are rejected and hurt or who suffer in some way for a just cause.[22] Whilst directed to his followers or disciples, this teaching binds together those of the Christian faith with those of other faiths and none. Together as we stand for what is right and just, as we stand against a corrupt system that keeps the poor, poor, we help to move the world closer to what we all desire… a world that is more compassionate, kind, valuing of the young and old, where people can experience peace, hope, meaning and prosperity. For those who follow the Christian faith we know this as a reflection of the Kingdom of heaven.

Whilst the beatitudes form part of Jesus' teaching to his disciples and so carry a spiritual component they also form a good checklist of psychological wellbeing for the community worker as they engage in personal and community transformation. In this way Jesus as liberator is concerned not only with our status before God in terms of ultimate salvation, but our health to engage with him in his continuing work of transformation.

The Role of the Holy Spirit

The Holy Spirit is perhaps the hardest member of the Trinity to understand and arguably has caused the most conflict between theologians and even denominations. The Holy Spirit applies Jesus work of liberation to us as individuals and is the guiding and empowering force of any good in the world. He/She is also the one who seals the effect of our work into an eternity that is tied up with God's ultimate plan to renew the world. Tom Wright shows that God brings people to faith through the work of his Spirit who then continues to lead them to follow Jesus, through discipleship but

---

22. Bonhoeffer, *Cost of Discipleship*, 113.

also through vocation. They are designed to be a sign and foretaste of what God wants to do for the entire cosmos. The exciting and hope filled reality is that these ones who come to faith are part of the means by which God renews the world in the present and ultimately in the future.[23]

Luke 4:18-21 begins with Jesus saying,

> "The Lord's Spirit
>   has come to me,
> because he has chosen me
> to tell the good news
>   to the poor.
> The Lord has sent me
> to announce freedom
>   for prisoners,
> to give sight to the blind,
> to free everyone
>   who suffers,
> [19] and to say, 'This is the year
>   the Lord has chosen.'"

> [20] Jesus closed the book, then handed it back to the man in charge and sat down. Everyone in the meeting place looked straight at Jesus.

> [21] Then Jesus said to them, "What you have just heard me read has come true today."

These verses show that the Spirit was present to empower Jesus for his mission in the world. Post his resurrection and before his ascension Jesus makes it clear to his disciples that he must leave in order for his Spirit to become available to his followers (John 14:25-26). Once the Spirit is present they will be empowered to do the same kind of things that Jesus did. Jesus' work and the work of his followers is the same and it all points towards a partial renewal of the world in the present and its eventual fulfilment in the future

The Spirit's role in the Trinity is to bring glory to Jesus. This is done through helping the believer to conform their will to the will of the liberator and thus join in the ongoing work of liberation as described in the verses above.[24]

---

23. Wright, *Surprised by Hope*, 212-213.

24. Millard J Erickson, *Christian Theology*, (Grand Rapids, MI: Baker Book House, 1983), 874.

Whilst not tangible in and of him/herself, the result of the Spirit's work is very evident in and through the believer.

Throughout biblical history the Spirit has had a number of roles. He/she was present at creation, hovering over the waters, helping to bring order out of chaos. The Spirit has been attributed with giving people prophetic insight, utterance and writing. Most Christians believe that the authors of the books of the Bible were inspired by the Spirit, and in fact the ordering of the canon is also believed to have been guided by the same Spirit. The Spirit also played a part in Jesus' conception, and was active in his life, descending onto him at his baptism.

Then finally the Spirit was made available for every believer. Here the issue of pneumatology really hots up. The first visible manifestation of the Spirit post Jesus' ascension was the outpouring evidenced by the followers speaking in tongues (Acts 2:1-13). In most instances in the Acts of the Apostles someone became a believer and then they were baptized in the Holy Spirit, allowing them to also speak in tongues. Although this was not always the case, there is one example of a community believing in Jesus but not immediately receiving the gift of the Spirit or at least the manifestation of tongues.

Regardless of how this all played out, since the early church there have been debates about the nature and role of the Holy Spirit, particularly around tongues and other manifestations such as miraculous healing. Those on the Pentecostal side of the debate believe that speaking in tongues is an essential sign of the presence of the Spirit. Others (a much smaller minority) believe that the gifts of the Spirit ended after the period of the early church. The mainstream Protestant belief about the Spirit has been affected by the rise of rationalism that sees all beliefs needing to be justified by reason. Because of the intangible nature of the Spirit this has caused his/her role to be minimized.

For our purposes, whilst the more 'miraculous' workings of the Holy Spirit are present in the Church today, including the work of regenerating the individual and helping them to become alive to God, the Spirit is active in more subtle but equally profound ways within the Church, the lives of believers and even more broadly in the world. Galatians 5 tells us that the fruits of the Spirit are joy, peace, patience, kindness, goodness, faithfulness, gentleness and self-control. Whether we are of the Christian faith or not it is possible to exhibit these qualities. (Warning: the next few lines could be offensive for those who don't share the faith.) However I believe that where these values are present, the Spirit of God is present. If we go back to what Christians refer to as the Fall (Genesis 3) we understand that each person was created in the image of God. The creation was marred by our collective choice to go our own path and not follow the way of life that God had hoped. This rebellion did not change the simple fact that the spark of the divine or the creator remained in each person. This spark, even though we may not be aware of it, allows us, if we choose, to live out the qualities listed in Galatians. If we adhere to the understanding that says God's spirit is present in the world and in each of us in this way, then we can take the view that humanity and ultimately this world is good. Over time debates have raged in the Christian church about whether humanity is ultimately bad or good. I fall in the latter camp and am hopeful that as we take hold of some of these truths we will grow more into the vision that God had when he created the world through the Spirit.

I'm not professing to know or understand how all of this works, however like Karl Rahner I believe there are anonymous Christians. He was particularly referring to people of other faiths, who through being devout would attain salvation and live in the grace of God.[25] For me I see that we partner with God, and that the Spirit is present, whenever we work for the values that he espouses. This means that not only people of faith but anyone who works for justice, mercy, equity, the rights of the marginalized and the betterment of the environment, who cares for the sick and hurting and fosters community, works towards God's picture of a renewed world, in the present and ultimately for the future. Eschatologically, whether those people get to experience the full benefit of a relationship with God, is up to him and outside the scope of this book.

So in concluding this section, the Holy Spirit is an equal part of the Trinity and works to bring glory to the Father and the Son. In the life of the believer this happens by the Spirit working to renew their heart and mind towards obedience to God's plan. The spark of the divine is evident in each person created by God. If they are willing the Spirit works, even unknown to the

---

25. Karl Rahner cited in Ross Langmeade, "Conviction and Openness: Dialogue and Witness in a Multifaith world" (Lecture presented as part of a subject, Contemporary Mission Theology: Contextualisation, Dialogue and Transformation, 9 April, 2008).

person, to enable them to display the fruits of the Spirit and to work towards a world where God's values are more evident.

Reflection Questions

1. How has your understanding of what God is doing through his Kingdom been stretched?

2. If your understanding has been stretched, how are you now seeing the role of Father, Son and Holy Spirit in the creation and maintaining of God's work in the world?

3. What connections can you see between people of faith and others who are working for similar outcomes as described in passages such as Isaiah 65?

4. When it comes to engagement with the world, how will you respond to the desires of the triune God?

Chapter 3. – A Model of God's Kingdom that We Can Embrace

If we only had eyes to see and ears to hear and wits to understand, we would know that the Kingdom of God in the sense of holiness, goodness, beauty is as close as breathing and is crying out to be born both within ourselves and within the world; we would know that the Kingdom of God is what we all of us hunger for above all other things even when we don't know its name or realize that its what we have been starving to death for. The Kingdom of God is where our best dreams come from and our truest prayers. We glimpse it at those moments when we find ourselves being better than we are and wiser than we know. We catch sight of it when at some moment of crisis a strength seems to come to us that is greater than our own strength. The Kingdom of God is where we belong. It is home, and whether we realize it or not, I think we are all of us homesick for it.

Frederick Buechner

Having briefly explored the nature and work of the Trinity, we are in a good position to begin to understand the different interpretations of the work of God's Kingdom in the world. From God's perspective the Kingdom is Trinitarian in nature and is both present in the world because of the work of Jesus, but is yet to come to its total fulfilment. Jesus' death, resurrection and ascension laid the foundation for the church, or ecclesia, which literally means a called out community. Empowered by the Spirit, the Church was to fulfil the mission of Jesus in the world, essentially being an eschatological community and an anticipatory sign of God's coming rule.[1] It will be helpful for us to have an understanding of the different models that have been built up in people's attempts to unpack what on earth (and beyond) God is doing. By working through these models we may be able to identify our own persuasion, that of our church and even others that we may seek to partner with. The Kingdom of God is the predominant paradigm used to understand God's work in the world. If this is true our understanding of it then becomes key for our missional endeavours.

---

1. Wolfhart Pannenberg, *Systematic Theology: Volume 3,* (Grand Rapids, MI: Eerdmans, 1997), 30.

Snyder's Eight Models of the Kingdom

In his book *Models of the Kingdom,* Howard Snyder explores a continuum of understanding about the Kingdom of God and its purposes in the world. He also sees that the Kingdom is the primary metaphor through which Christians have understood what it means to believe in Christ and through him be related to God and the world.[2] Snyder has delineated eight points along the continuum, from which to construct models. In this instance a model is understood to be a representation or a sum up of a number of perspectives that fit coherently together. Each have elements of the truth, yet on their own don't tell the whole story. The predominant model in any given time or place varied depending on whether the Church was experiencing persecution, hardship or times of influence. They include seeing the Kingdom as: predominantly future hope, an inner spiritual experience, a mystical communion, the Church, a counter-system, a political state, Christianized culture, an earthly utopia. The models mainly relate to the nature (inner spiritual reality vs broader influence) and timing (present vs future) of the impact of the Kingdom. Snyder concludes that the better models hold together six biblical tensions or paradoxes and that they fail to the extent that they try to resolve these tensions.

To a greater or lesser extent these models form the basis of today's belief regarding the Kingdom. Subtly a church's belief about the Kingdom - the core place of its influence, how it will be fulfilled, how it relates to the individual and the corporate reality of the church - will determine where that church puts its energy and how open it will be to different sorts of mission and community engagement. Thankfully this is beginning to change. However, modern examples of conservative Protestantism have largely seen the Kingdom as an internal, personal reality with very little to offer broader society. This way of thinking contains the view that when Jesus returns he will usher in a new heaven and a new earth that will do away with all the existing structures and the materiality of this world. This belief holds inherent in its walls that ultimately we are made for a disembodied afterlife, rather than focusing on a bodily resurrection and a renewing of earth when the full reign of God finally appears. If one's belief is that all we see will be done away with and we will live with God in Heaven, in terms of mission the preoccupation will be with saving souls, rather than working

---

2.   Howard Snyder, *Models of the Kingdom,* (Nashville, TN: Abingdon Press, 1991), 22.

for a renewed humanity, seen as the sign of the Kingdom's presence with us now.

Ten years ago Australian media personality and agnostic Andrew Denton produced a documentary called *God on My Side*. It was based on delegates attending the 63rd National Religious Broadcasters Convention in Texas. Denton's respectful curiosity allowed him a unique view of the delegates. His exposé depicted a focused theology that revolved around an understanding of this world as evil and that the end times would see a dramatic second coming of Christ, a literal new Jerusalem and the final judgment of humanity. There was very little room for renewal outside of these events.

Whilst this view maybe too simplistic to encompass all who attended the convention, it highlights a particular understanding of God's Kingdom and therefore our responsibility as followers of Christ. The models we are about to explore will shed some light on this example as well as other views of mission and church that we may have come across.

Future Hope

Our first stop on Snyder's continuum of Kingdom understanding is the future hope model. This idea is based on cosmic reconciliation. Essentially Christ will return and usher in the new heaven and the new earth before which time he will have ruled for a thousand years. At this point all evil will also be judged (Titus 2:13, Matt 24:14, Isa 24:21-23). This model carries with it a general pessimism towards the current state of the world, seeing no hope of transformation before the second coming. Whilst lacking an understanding of God's grace for the present order, the model holds to a wonderful hope of what the future with God will be like (Isa 65:17-25). A core belief of proponents of this model is the need to preach the gospel to the whole world, which will usher in Christ's return.[3] Typically individual Christians and churches that hold fast to this view see very little point in getting involved in the messy task of building community or caring for the poor. Quite often if they do get involved it is only as a means to an end, quite clearly seeing any work apart from the literal speaking of the gospel as periphery at the best and a waste of time at the worst.

---

3.   Snyder, *Models of the Kingdom*, Chapter 2.

Inner Spiritual Connection

Proponents of the second model see the Kingdom as an inner spiritual experience (Luke 17:20-21). Teresa of Avila is perhaps the strongest advocate for this model and wrote about her creation of an interior castle. She understood salvation as participation in God and emphasized the individual's spiritual experience with the real world being the realm of the Spirit. She drew on mystical images such as light and fire seeing God's nature as an immense sea. Charles Wesley would later go on to draw on some of her imagery. According to this model, life is essentially spiritual and non-material (2 Pet 1:4, Col 1:27, Eph 3:17-19, Heb 6:19-20). The key difference between this model and the next one, mystical communion, is the degree in which this experience is shared with others in community. According to Snyder's second model, signs of the Kingdom aren't evident in the world or society but are part of an inner consciousness or participation in God. This model is Platonic in its origins and sets up an unhelpful dichotomy between the spiritual and the material. It sets the primary role of the church to provide access to the Spiritual Kingdom. Like the first model it has considerable biblical and historical support and is a counter to the secularization of the gospel. However it is not always clear on its understanding of the role of Jesus and has elements akin to new age thinking, including a weighty focus on individualism that creates isolation from other Christians. Finally, as the model relates to our context of community engagement, it runs counter to much of the social thrust of the prophets of the Old Testament and Jesus himself.[4]

Mystical Communion

Snyder's third model is the understanding of the Kingdom as mystical communion with all believers. This spiritual connection is present with believers throughout the ages, and forms an invisible corporate reality, that is not bound by space or time. The ultimate hope of mystical communion is that it will be fulfilled when the Kingdom comes in all its glory. The Church is seen to partake spiritually in this union in the present and in this way reflects the Kingdom and Christ's glory (Eph 2:21-22). Jesus on the Mount of Transfiguration (Luke 9:28-36) is the central image of this model, its fulfilment is visible in the last supper because of the believers' connection through the body of Christ. God dwells with the Christian community, both

---

4.   Snyder, *Models of the Kingdom*, Chapter 3.

those in the present and the past. The focus of the Church's worship is the heavenly realm (Kingdom) under God's leadership. The worship is highly sacramental, both symbolizing and actualizing the mystery of communion with God and the mystical body of Christ. The presence of the Kingdom is a foretaste of heaven with the ultimate reality being in the next world. The primary agent of the Kingdom is God with the Spirit working through the sacraments or means of grace, such as prayer. In this way a worshipping and praying community visibly models the Kingdom of Heaven.

The Kingdom as mystical communion stands in opposition to the world, the flesh and the devil, seeing them as obstacles on the path to heaven. The material world, including passions, need to be overcome by spiritual discipline. Saints are encouraged in this through participation in heavenly community. This will culminate in everlasting worship of God in Heaven (Rev 4-7). As with the other two models it has strengths and weaknesses. The model rests in a narrow biblical basis with limited scriptural truth. There is an over-spiritualization of reality and the promised Kingdom. Any compromise to this is seen as secularization, despite the Bible's talk of a material reality and a 'this worldly' aspect to God's reign. As such the model displays very little hope of positive social change and cancels out the motivation to see the Kingdom in the social order. Whilst being less individual than the second model it still falls prey of a Platonic dualism. It does however present a counterbalance to a materialistic church and has a strong experimental flavour. The Kingdom is not a disembodied future hope, but is a deeply personal, shared experience.[5]

Church Equals Kingdom

The fourth stop along the Kingdom continuum is where the Church and the Kingdom are equated as the same thing. At least where the Church is a present manifestation of the Kingdom. A significant strand of Christianity has held this view. Matthew 16:18-19 links the Church and Kingdom, even providing elements of authority. God is seen to reign on the earth through the Church and particularly through the structures of authority. The visible Church therefore is a sign, symbol and ultimately the representation of God's invisible reign over all things. The Church and Kingdom are therefore linked conceptually and theologically, the Church is seen as the present visible form of the Kingdom, and authority structures and the Church's

---

5.   Snyder, *Models of the Kingdom*, Chapter 4.

authoritative claims are in focus. Metaphors like the City of God and royal priesthood (1Pet 2:4-9) shows God's people as a Kingdom, with Israel under David and Solomon seen as a paradigm (Ps 29:10-11).

The visible Church is seen as the custodian and embodiment of God's reign, with a high respect for Christians who are in positions of social, political and economic influence. The clergy are seen as the Lord's anointed and there is a clear distinction between the clergy and laity. God is believed to be present in the life and experience of the Church, with the building itself seen as a sacred space. Signs of the Kingdom's presence are the success and growth of the church. The opponents of the Kingdom are seen to be satanic and demonic forces, anything that opposes the Church.

This model is prevalent when the Church is successful or dominant in society, when it is at home in the culture having developed influence and prestige. It was the predominant understanding of the Catholic Church in the West, with the Pope being seen as the vicar of Jesus Christ. However, the Catholic Church has shifted to a more transformational view of the Kingdom. Meanwhile Protestantism tends to confuse the work of the Church and the work of the Kingdom, the two are often seen as the same with the present Kingdom being reduced to the dimensions of the Church. The Protestant Church in the US often defaults to this model (with a mix of others) with it playing a part in the development of a cultural religiosity. This model has led to confusion between what it means to grow the Church and grow the Kingdom, with many equating a growth in numbers with growing the Kingdom. Equating Kingdom and Church leads to questions about the nature of God's mission and the expected effect of evangelism.[6]

As mentioned, if the two are equated, the only valid mission is to grow the Church through evangelism. However, appropriate distance and separation between the two allows for a broader, more holistic interpretation of mission. One that includes the recognition of an individual's vocation and the spaces and places that God has created them to be in.

Kingdom growth can include being elected to the city council. David, a good friend and mentor of mine, spent four amazing years on Melbourne's City Council. He was given the community services portfolio and amongst other things instituted a monthly lunch with people experiencing homelessness. This led to a trip to the US and the exploration of a new

---

6.   Snyder, *Models of the Kingdom,* Chapter 5.

model of holistic housing. The model included safe accommodation, medical and community services on site and a range of spaces for people to mix and build relationships.

A Counter-System

The fifth model is the understanding of the Kingdom as a counter-system or an alternative way of organizing society. The Kingdom is seen as distinct from the church and is subversive, seeking to replace the dominant values of the society. It is seen to be in opposition to the powers of the present age. There are four core features of this model;

1. Prophetic Character: Following the Biblical call to seek first the Kingdom, which is essentially an invitation to live life in harmony with God's values, including working for the creation of a just society.

2. Strongly Christocentric: The model calls the Christian community to live out the ethics of Jesus as part of what it means to be a disciple. Jesus is seen as the centre, model and foundation of the Christian community as it seeks to be a missionary minority in society.

3. Call to be counter cultural: The Christian community in faithfulness to Jesus Christ is to live counter to the predominant values of the society.

4. Peaceable Kingdom: The community of faith is to trust God for victory and not take up arms against an oppressor. This is to be a sign of God's reign and a new order of peace of justice.

A core image for this model is the vision of the triumphant lamb in Revelation. This is both the culmination of the Kingdom and a provider of hope and direction for the faithful community in their present time. The counter-system the Church is to employ is not essentially about revolution. However, it is based on the subversive ideal of servanthood and sacrifice, modelled by Jesus (Matt 20:25-28; Mark 8:35-38, 10:29-31). According to the fifth model, Jesus also teaches that ultimately his Kingdom is not of this world, so bearing arms is not necessary (John 18:36). This model also draws its scriptural basis from the Old Testament, pointing to images of Shalom and the importance of justice in this present time. It's important to this model that the church is seen as a suffering minority and it has had prevalence at times when the church has been under persecution.[7]

John Howard Yoder encapsulates the model, seeing that the church is to live now what ultimately the world is called to be, in this way it lives as a microcosm of the wider society. Throughout history there have been a number of periods and groups who have more or less adopted this understanding. They include Francis of Assissi who called for the Church to live out the radical nature of the Kingdom. This included brothers in his order not acquiring property, money or goods; they were to serve the Lord in poverty and humility. In this way Francis was seen as a reformer, embracing the foundations of church tradition, modelling what the Kingdom of God meant in everyday life. Other groups to adopt variations of this understanding include the Anabaptists and some strains of Latin American liberation theology.

As with all the models there are positives and negatives. The Kingdom as counter-system has a negative view of human culture and is passive towards political and other types of societal influence, encouraging the church, rather to be that alternative culture. The model is also criticized for its anti-institutional flavour and for being naïve about the need for social structures. It fails to see that God can work through those structures and that renewal movements often start at the margins of society and continue to form in its cracks. On the positive side of the ledger the Kingdom as counter-system holds a prophetic power and sees that an alternative life is possible and can be lived now. It has considerable biblical support, particularly its focus on Jesus' life and the call to discipleship. The joint foci of seeing Jesus as the key to the Kingdom and the church as a social community leaves the door open for a new social reality where Christians can share life together day by day. The Church's witness to the world is to humbly serve, not force values on the world, in the full assurance that God will bring the Kingdom in his time and his way. The model holds together a few important tensions, namely the individual and social reality of the Kingdom, and its present and future nature as well as its gentleness and power (Rev 5:5-6).

Religion and Politics

Snyder's sixth model is the Kingdom as political state. Proponents of this model believe that the present rule of God is through the structures of

---

7. Snyder, *Models of the Kingdom,* Chapter 6.

human government. In this theocratic view God's Kingdom provides the values and even a methodology for the organizing of the major aspects of society. Ideally this rule is not a democracy but one where the righteous rule in the name of God. It is a present rule though not visible or manifest in its totality; it will grow and flower when God takes dominion over all things. This model revolves around the second coming of Christ when he will take control of all things. The Kingdom as political state has three characteristics;

1. Old Testament Law: That biblical morality ought to be the foundation for all civil law.

2. Authority of God: He is seen as judge and ruler, the phrase Kingdom of God is taken more literally than in other models.

3. Optimism: That there will be a growing influence of the Church in the world.

Some who adhere to this model see that human kind will be converted or alternatively that the Church will remain the minority but rule politically as God's agents as the Kingdom of God is established on earth. There is debate around how this will happen, either by the Church ruling in society as in the time of Christendom or through Christian political leaders. Adherents to this understanding of the Kingdom see its signs as righteousness (morality) in society and God's blessing of prosperity on his people. The enemies are seen as satanic forces as well as any power that opposes God's laws.

This model is seen in the Old Testament through the reign of Kings David and Solomon, who had a strong personal faith in God and became his instruments to lead his people. Throughout history the model became prevalent with the conversion of Constantine in 322CE and the associated political structure. It was felt the Kingdom of God had come to earth with the rise of Byzantine Christianity and the founding of Constantinople, the new Rome in 330CE. Calvin also embodied this model as he attempted to set up the reign of God in Geneva. He wanted to establish a Holy Commonwealth where God ruled and there was a parallelism between the church and the state. However in reality he was unable to establish a true theocracy with the elected council being viewed as a legitimate God ordained authority, but not truly the reign of God.

Other reformers to take on aspects of this model include Bucer (1491-1551CE) who wanted a complete reform of church and society in England.

He saw the Kingdom as a Christocracy and was looking for the reign of Christ's spirit in every area of society. He possessed an optimism based in God's grace that both Luther and Calvin lacked. Some saw his thinking in line with Plato's play called Republic where a city is ruled by philosopher-kings. Rather, he saw a logical outworking of the biblical truth that community leaders in both the church and state had to promote. Oliver Cromwell (1599-1658CE), a political figure in England, who established a form of democracy, longed for a literal theocracy and interpreted Daniel 7 as God about to set up a fifth empire following the Babylonian, Persian, Greek and Roman empires. This empire would be centred in England, through which the saints would rule the earth. To a greater extent America was also founded on the dream of a theocracy, with different strains of Christianity such as the Puritans, Pilgrims of Plymouth, Quakers, German sectarians, Dutch reformed and Presbyterians, all promoting a slightly different understanding of what it meant for the Kingdom of God to be present and for a theocracy to be established. In time there would also be a number of movements started on North American soil.

One of the more interesting attempts at establishing a theocracy happened in China during the Taiping Revolution of the 1850s. Hong Xiuquan (1814-1864CE) was a poor Chinese scholar who learned about the Christian faith through tracts given out by the Protestant missionary Robert Morrison. Hong saw himself as a special emissary from God, the second Christ, sent to establish a heavenly kingdom of eternal peace and prosperity. He was a charismatic leader and made many converts forming the Society of God Worshippers. He raised a large people's army and in a few years gained control of half of China. He attempted to drive Manchus from power and establish a capital in Nanjing. He ruled for a decade, with this time being seen as the first chapter in China's revolutionary struggle. Hong possessed a basic understanding of Scripture and had a clear vision of God as heavenly king and father, with Jesus Christ as the son who died to redeem the world from sin. However, he focused more on the Old Testament seeing God as a lawgiver, took the concept of the fatherhood of God literally, and rejected the doctrine of the Holy Spirit. He saw God's Kingdom as a literal theocracy with a moralistic and legalistic focus. Hong did not succeed in taking over China and is remembered negatively by many due to the fifteen years of military struggle and the millions of lives that were lost in his attempt to set up a theocracy.[8]

A Cultural Outworking

The Kingdom as Christianized Culture is stop 7 on Snyder's continuum of models. The proponents of this model see that the Kingdom has a stimulus and program for the transformation of society. The Kingdom is already present although only in part. As such it is the inspiration and direction for the Christians working towards positive change. The Kingdom is understood to be present, broader than the individual, and contains a material reality, not just a spiritual one. The role of the Church is to work towards social transformation, not create a Christian enclave as the sixth model suggests. In one of his parables Jesus describes the Kingdom as a leavening agent, such as yeast. Those who adhere to the seventh model understand the message of this story as pointing to the need for Christian values to permeate all of society. In this way the Kingdom illuminates mankind progressively over time, overcoming fear and ignorance, ushering in a better world. There are three key features of this model:

1. Relevance: The work of the Kingdom is seen much broader than the Church, as God's intention is to redeem every aspect of society. This brings a strong ethical focus and a living out of the moral values of the Kingdom.

2. Transformation: The Kingdom's work is focused on social, political and economic realities and processes. God's Kingdom has a social program and there is a logical and necessary outworking of Jesus' teachings.

3. Optimism: The belief that social transformation is possible and that the gospel can be a force for peace and harmony. This includes the hope of justice in our world including just governmental structures and an equitable society.

For these things to be achieved the model recognizes the need for God and humankind to work co-operatively, and in this way the Kingdom becomes progressively manifest in the present order. This in contrast to the models that see the Kingdom coming in the future, solely by God's hand. In our media soaked society we are often led to believe that the world is a dark and

---

8.   Snyder, *Models of the Kingdom,* Chapter 7.

horrible place, with very little hope of things getting better. Whilst there are many negatives, there are also signs of hope in key areas such as climate change, crime rates (particularly around violent crimes) and justice issues. As the Old Testament prophets lamented, there is still much work to be done (Isa 11:1-9; 42:1-7, 61:1-11), however there are many current signs of the presence of God's Kingdom. The New Testament holds only a few references to the outworking of this model. However, Jesus' teaching on the Kingdom and his social ethics provide a pathway to be followed. This model holds the tension between evangelism and social reform as central themes in the manifestation of the Kingdom.[9]

Utopias: Can they ever work?

Model eight presents an interesting conundrum, describing the Kingdom as an earthly utopia. Most of the proponents of the model envision this utopia from a humanistic viewpoint, effectively wanting the outcome of a brighter better world without the accompanying spirituality. E. Stanley Jones sees that this is impossible and that if we ignore the presence of the Kingdom it will only lead to self-frustration and self-destruction.[10] Have you ever had the experience of something from inside you gnawing at you? From the outside everything looks normal, but you know something is not right or even missing. From personal experience I've discovered if you don't connect in with that feeling there is a lot of frustration and even self-destructive patterns that can emerge. Jones believes this is similar in society if we try to reproduce the Kingdom, leaving God out of the mix. Whilst I believe that where we see the values of God at work, the Kingdom is present, it is impossible to bring a better world into its full potential without God. Model eight has a range of responses to Jesus. Some see him as irrelevant, others as the cosmic Christ of goodwill.[11] Or in fact he might be held up as a paradigm of what is being worked towards. The Kingdom is seen as earthly and again the church can be seen as the organization that embodies the ethics and values of the Kingdom, or can be irrelevant as in Communism. The final goal is seen as a perfect, harmonious balanced society on earth.[12]

---

9. Snyder, *Models of the Kingdom*, Chapter 8.

10. E. Stanley Jones, *Is The Kingdom of God Realism?*, (New York, NY: Abingdon, 1940), 59-63.

11. Snyder, *Models of the Kingdom*, 119.

12. Snyder, *Models of the Kingdom*, Chapter 9.

Models one to eight are on a continuum and as such model eight has a similar outcome to the first model, although the methodology and actualization of how this comes about is vastly different.

Assessing the Models

As Snyder points out, no one model encompasses the whole truth. We've taken this journey through the various models of the Kingdom to illustrate the diversity at which the Christian faith and others understand the work of the Kingdom in the world. When I'm taking my students through this material I start by asking them what they think is important to God. Inevitably we produce a whiteboard full of words and concepts that encompass much of what we experience on a daily basis. The challenge to them then is, if all these things are important to God and encompass aspects of the Kingdom, why do we act as though there are only two things that really matter to God? Those being firstly salvation and secondly what happens within the walls of our particular expression of church. I know these are generalizations. However, held within these understandings are the models of the Kingdom we have come to own.

Why is all this important? If we own a model or conglomeration of models that limits our understanding to salvation and the interior workings of any particular church then this will seriously hamper our motivation to be involved in a broader, more encompassing model of mission that includes community development.

Snyder points out the more accurate models of the Kingdom embrace and hold in tension a number of what on the surface can appear competing biblical elements: individual vs corporate, spiritual vs material, gradual vs climactic (relating to Christ's role in end times), divine vs human action and the nature of and relationship between church and Kingdom.

The selection of models that help us hold these tensions as well as allow room for God's broad agenda in the world is model seven, with aspects of models two and three.

Model seven supposes that God intended for the Kingdom to have a real impact in the present order. It argues that God has a model for communities and societies based on a universal set of values and principles, found in Scripture and outworked in various ways through history. God does not attempt to instil these values alone, seeking to work in cooperation with human action. Whilst ultimately only God can bring about the fullness of the new creation in the bringing of heaven to earth, we are to be like the son, living out and teaching the social ethics that can be found in the gospels. Baptist theologian Walter Rauschenbusch demonstrated that this understanding of the Kingdom brought about the split between the social gospel and fundamentalists. Many felt that the basic tenants of the faith were being down played and that the focus should be the salvation of the individual.[13]

Tom Wright picks this up, arguing that God's intention from Genesis to Revelation is justice. A fundamentalism that says the world is in such a mess that nothing can be done about it until Jesus returns, is a form of dualism. Like the Sadducees, many fundamentalists are threatened by the depiction of a Jesus who brings the future into the present and calls his followers to work and pray for a greater realization of that future.[14]

Models two and three help us to balance this. Whilst God works broader than those who make up the Church, that is, he is present wherever his values are manifest, as an expression of ultimate reality, he predominantly works through those who have had a personal encounter with him. If this were not the case, then a common model of the Kingdom would be an earthly utopia. Model two talks of the Kingdom as inner spiritual experience. Taken to its extreme it sets up a dichotomy between spirit and matter. However, an inner transformation is needed for a person to experience the full reality of the Kingdom. Model three is mystical communion. Whilst not adopting the mystical aspects in their entirety, the model helps us to see that the experience of transformation does not happen in isolation and that the Kingdom is a corporate reality. The Church is a communion of the saints both past and present and there is an element of mystery around all of this.[15]

The impact of the Kingdom, therefore, is inner and personal in as much as a believer is transformed by the power of the Spirit, or in Wright's words, becomes part of the new creation. By the Spirit the new creation is drawn together into a community. That community is given a task of being agents of Kingdom focused transformation. Again, in Wright's words, they are to

---

13. Snyder, *Models of the Kingdom*, 104-107.
14. Wright, *Surprised by Hope*, 224-226.
15. Snyder, *Models of the Kingdom*, Chapter 3 and 4.

build for the Kingdom and to look forward with hope, that what they are building will go into eternity, making up parts of the new heaven and the new earth, which will be revealed fully when the Kingdom comes in its final consummation.[16]

Kingdom Inspired Building of A Better World

Throughout the period of the Christian faith there have been many examples of those that have applied the values and principles we have been exploring to help make the world a better place. They may not articulate it in the same way but nevertheless were and are building for the Kingdom, working on the foundation that Jesus laid with his death and resurrection and joining him in renewing the world.

Dietrich Bonhoeffer

Bonhoeffer, whose look at the Beatitudes we focused on earlier, was born in Breslau, Prussia in 1906, dying at the hands of the Nazis in 1945 as the regime was collapsing at the end of the Second World War. He was a Lutheran pastor, writer/theologian and Nazi dissident. He wrote a number of influential texts about the Church's role in the world. As part of his resistance to the Nazi regime he loudly opposed Hitler's euthanasia program and his persecution of the Jews. Along with members of his family he would later be part of an assassination plot to kill Hitler.

Fundamental to his later actions was his time in America. As a twenty-four year old he went to teach at Union Theological Seminary where he was introduced to the Abyssinian Baptist Church, a black church in Harlem. It was there he heard Adam Clayton Powell Sr. preach on the Gospel of Social Justice. Through these experiences he became sensitive to social injustices, both the oppression of African Americans and the Church's inability to integrate. He began to see things from below, from the view of the oppressed.

It was this understanding that he took with him as he established a seminary for training Confessing Church pastors in Finkenwalde, Germany. Because of his outspoken opposition to the Nazi party his authorization to teach at the University of Berlin was revoked and he was labelled a pacifist and enemy of the state. Despite this he found funding and established the training school, only to have it shut a few years later in September 1937.

16. Wright, *Surprised by Hope,* 219.

He was not swayed from his mission to teach confessional theology tinged with the social gospel and spent two years secretly traveling from one East German village to the next. He continued to attract the attention of the Gestapo, but managed to join the Abwehr, a Germany military intelligence organization. The organization hoped that Bonhoeffer could help establish international relations for a post-war Germany. In time they deemed it right to attempt to assassinate Hitler. This attempt failed and Bonhoeffer along with other members of his family lost their lives.

Bonhoeffer taught and lived the importance of sacrifice for the poor and the oppressed. He stood fast to his beliefs, seeking a world of justice and equality. His writings continue to be influential in shaping what true discipleship looks like in the face of a potentially hostile world.

The Branken Family

Despite the end of Apartheid over twenty years ago, South Africa is still a very divided country with white people making up around 9% of the population yet controlling almost 80% of the wealth. Nelson Mandela, with his ability to bring the country together, took incredible steps towards justice, however in many respects this move seems to have stalled. There are still massive inequalities evidenced in the health and education systems as well as in housing and wages. On a recent trip to South Africa I was astounded by middle class streets lined with high intimidating fences of all varieties and gated communities with security guards stationed on the roads into the community. Houses in these areas are owned almost exclusively by white people, with black South Africans only present as domestic help. Contrast this with Hillbrow, an inner city suburb of Johannesburg, a mostly coloured community that has a mix of black South Africans and people who have come from countries like Zimbabwe, looking for work and a place to call home. The majority of people live in dilapidated high-rise flats, often run by 'pirates,' who exploit the poor with high rents.

Enter into this environment Nigel and Trish Branken, along with their now six children. They moved from a comfortable middle class existence, where Nigel was a social worker, to a flat in Hillbrow. Their desire is to see a world where people are valued more than things and where rich people join forces with others to see an end to inequality and extreme poverty. When they arrived, the Branken family did not pretend that they had the answers to all of Hilbrow's problems. In fact the opposite was true. They humbly moved into the community and began a journey of change. First, in the sentiments of Ghandi, putting effort into the journey of personal change and transformation through leaving themselves vulnerable to be hurt again and again by the pain and heartache they witnessed around them. As relationships grew they have been able to build a team of locals who help in various works that the Brankens have initiated. These include a homework club, weekly visits to friends on the street, community meals, and, most recently, bringing together a group of people to dream about Hilbrow's future.

During my time with the Brankens I was impacted by their love for those around them and their desire for justice. One morning I joined Nigel and a couple of the team as we went to witness women lining up for medical attention at a nearby clinic. Two hours before the clinic opened the line was already around the block. When the clinic did eventually open many of the women would be told it was too full for them to be seen. This was not just a random visit. Nigel had organized for a local media intern to accompany us, as she was interested in publicizing stories of injustice, particularly those involving women. Advocacy is a key part of what Nigel does, putting his concerns for his country on a local and global stage through social media. What is most striking about this family though is their love - for each other, but reaching beyond the family to welcome those that are downtrodden and hurting in whatever way.

This love was particularly evident as I went with Trish to visit friends who lived in downtown Johannesburg. Because of the huge numbers of people experiencing homelessness, unscrupulous businessmen are free to charge high rents and offer very little in return. We drove into what looked like a converted multi storey car park or gutted factory. We drove up to the first floor and waited for the gate to be opened. Once parked, Trish led the way through a darkened maze of corridors, each side lined with flimsy walls and doors. Behind each door was a family. The rooms consisted of bedding, usually bunks, and perhaps a cupboard and cooking ring. There was no running water in the rooms and the lighting was extremely dull. Smaller than the size of an average bedroom, these rooms often housed families up to nine people. Trish was here to visit a friend who was going into business and needed some help attending to the finer details. Whilst there she checked in with a number of others. The smiles were huge as the people received Trish, offered her hospitality and welcomed me.

Nigel, Trish and their children believe in a South Africa that looks more like God's Kingdom and are prepared to give their own pursuits for a more comfortable life away for that goal.

Jarrod McKenna

Jarrod, his wife Teresa and son Tyson live in a suburb of Perth in Western Australia. Jarrod is a pastor and an activist, and works with World Vision as their National Advisor on Faith and Activism. The couple were the first in history to crowd-source their mortgage. The dream behind this was to create a space where they could co-live with and empower refugees. This now takes place with a household of twenty in a space that used to be a drug den.

Jarrod is also responsible for the *Love Makes A Way* campaign. This has seen over two hundred church leaders occupy the offices of federal parliamentarians in an effort to have all children of asylum seekers freed from Australian immigration detention centres. Jarrod has been arrested four times in the past year for this stand on justice. Remarkably, the arresting officers have been supportive of the cause and magistrates have exonerated the group. All their demonstrations and occupancies have been peaceful, with the single focus of the children being released. Other advocacy campaigns have taken place through Common Grace and have focused on economic and environmental justice.

Previously Jarrod headed up the Peace Tree Community, a modern expression of Anabaptist principles, working with some of the poorest communities in Perth. In 2007 there was a gang killing between two ethnic groups and there was fear of race riots and reciprocity. The Peace Tree Community's first response was to gather in prayer. Creativity flowed and they took chalk to the local streets, writing sayings like 'something must change.' After further prayer one of the members suggested they organize a community wide gathering called 'Pizza for Peace.' The community, including those from the two ethnic groups involved in the killing, were invited. The Peace Tree Community led a time of prayer for an end to violence both locally and in the world. They planted an almond tree to remember the victim's life and invited those closest to him to put soil on the base of the tree as a prayer for remembrance and healing.

Through all of these experiences Jarrod holds to a simple faith as the basis of his actions, seeing that God loved him so much that he gave himself for him and rose again, and that we are invited to live that love.

Kingdom Reflections

It might be simple but living this love involves sacrifice as it did for Bonhoeffer, the Branken family and the McKennas. Whilst living in very different circumstances, each had and, for the latter two, still have a clear vision of what the world could be and are determined to demonstrate that vision in and through their lives. The three are joined by a commitment to the poor and marginalized, recognizing that each person has something unique to offer and that they possess the spark of the divine waiting to be fanned into flame.

Throughout the last two chapters we have explored the three in oneness of God and the roles of each member of the Trinity. God the Father as creator and sustainer, God the Son as liberator and the one who transforms, and God the Holy Spirit who personalizes Jesus' work and is the force behind any good in the world. Each was followed by an example of their work or how it is applied to us. In chapter three we explored various models of the Kingdom of God, the ultimate expression and work of the Trinity in the world. The most helpful understanding of the Kingdom in the world is a combination of Snyder's model seven with sub models two and three. This enables us to see the Kingdom of God as having a blueprint for the way communities, cities and indeed society as a whole can function, as well as recognizing that the Kingdom meets the individual and the Church both now and in the past, linking all believers together. These models also hold in tension the now and not yet aspects of the Kingdom, showing a gradual (greater expression in the world now) and climactic coming of the Kingdom, when Jesus returns. Linking the blueprint idea and Snyder's second and third model also allows room to recognize that God is present in the life of the individual believer and that of the Church.

The Church has a unique role to play in the outworking of God's Kingdom. Not an exclusive role, but a unique one! The next chapter will explore the shape and role of the Church necessary for it to respond to God's Kingdom in the world. Following which I will seek to unpack the journey to our current Western culture, through the Renaissance and ending with an exposé of postmodernism. Then we will begin to look more practically at our world and the tools necessary for us to engage with the poor and marginalized and build communities more generally.

Reflection Questions

1. How does the quote by Frederick Buechner at the start of the chapter fuel your passion for mission?
2. Before reading this chapter what would have been your primary understanding of the Kingdom? (Pick one main model with aspects from one to two secondary models.)
3. What's changed after reading the chapter?
4. What did you find inspiring about the individuals I highlighted who are following a Kingdom dream as they work towards a better world?

Chapter 4. - The Church, Partnering with God

Social responsibility becomes an aspect not of Christian mission only, but also of Christian conversion. It is impossible to be truly converted to God without being thereby converted to our neighbour.

John R.W. Stott

Inclusion: it was always part of the plan

It was a dry and dusty day, like most other days in the desert. The midday sun was beating down on the heads of the hired workers. They had just stopped to fetch water from a nearby well to refresh the sheep and goats being herded along the road. The men were also able to have a drink and the cool water meeting the parched back of throats brought instant relief. There was plenty to go around so heads and faces were splashed and scarves wet. As the journey continued, in the shimmery distance the men saw, like an apparition, a flaming bush, yet the bush didn't seem to burn down. With caution they approached this most unusual sight. Suddenly one of their number took off his sandals and moved quickly towards the bush.

The full story of Moses and the burning bush can be read in Exodus 3 and is one of the key passages that show God setting the Israelites apart as a nation to be governed by him. Over the years many have taken this as an indication of exclusivity and in turn have looked to the Church to carry on the legacy of being God's people. This has led to an inward focus and a faulty understanding of the doctrine of election. Traditional understandings teach that Israel and in turn those who become Christians are God's elect and everyone else is not. This has led some to take up a frenzied attitude toward evangelism, believing that the elect in each generation must be discovered. Others have become complacent about evangelism and indeed anything else that happens in this world believing that it is all transitory and that the real world is yet to come. Whilst that might be comforting to believe at times, it is false and leads to a dangerous indifference to the poor and the state of the world.

The doctrine of election is more to do with some being chosen to be a blessing to others. The Old Testament is quite clear that Israel was meant to be an example to the nations of how life could be. That is what life looks like, being devoted to God. Passages that describe shalom and the jubilee

71

laws, which talk of flourishing and restoration, point to a rich full life for all. Unfortunately Israel became tied up with their own sense of importance and rebellion against God, which meant they didn't follow the pathways to these opportunities.

God's desire to be inclusive continued over into the New Testament, and whilst Jesus almost exclusively worked within the Jewish community, his intent was to instil within his disciples the DNA of God's desire that all would find life and be able to live it to the full. Pentecost, with its arrival and indwelling of the Holy Spirit, signaled the birth of the Church and with its display of people speaking in different languages showed once again God's commitment to inclusivity. God's desire for all his creation to be connected to him was once again shown in Acts when the hapless Peter was invited to the household of Cornelius, a Roman soldier. Previous to the invitation, Peter had a dream where he was being shown a sheet full of different food which, according to the Jewish food laws, was unclean. God challenged Peter to eat. At first he refused, with God eventually saying not to call unclean what he called clean. When Cornelius' men arrived and asked Peter to go with them, as difficult as the paradigm shift was, he was able to accept the invitation and welcomed Cornelius and his household into the family of faith.

Paul furthered this acceptance by being seen as the Apostle to the Gentiles, travelling over large parts of the known world. He preached and demonstrated the good news, not only the truth about Jesus, but the effect his death and resurrection had for us and its possibilities for the world. Jesus' resurrection opened the door for all humankind to participate in his dream for the world. Which can be summed up in the concept of shalom, a holistic Hebrew greeting that seeks wellbeing for all of life.

To help unpack this concept and our role in it, we will explore what has shaped our understanding of the universal Church and how a local expression can best prepare itself to be bearers of the shalom image and create a pathway to be effectively involved in community engagement.

Unpacking the Universal Church

There have been many books written on this subject, space does not allow us the room to do an in-depth analysis and I can't hope to add to the work of ecclesiological scholars. My aim is simply to outline a few points which highlights the Church's mission DNA. German systematic theologian

Wolfhart Pannenberg writes on the Church and the Kingdom. His view of the Kingdom is limited to essentially an inner and future perspective, seeing essentially that God works through his people, but that the reality of the Kingdom won't truly be present until Christ comes again. Whilst this is limiting, Pannenberg's work on the Church is helpful for our context, particularly his thoughts on what binds it together.

In Australia and throughout the world there are various movements that focus on the unity of the Church. They encourage churches of all denominations to come together, essentially for prayer and to worship together. I have been a part of a couple of these movements, one focused in such a way, the other more focused on helping the combined church in an area engage with it's community. Whilst I believe coming together for prayer is important, a mistake that can tend to be made, probably more in the former than the latter, is that unity becomes the goal. The feeling is that if the Church in a city comes together in unity and prays, then God will be more likely to send revival. Whilst there is at least anecdotal evidence to spur this thinking on, ecclesiologically it is not helpful, as having unity as the end goal tends to enhance the inward focus of the Church to the detriment of its outward mission.

This kind of thinking is also theologically inaccurate, as the Church is already unified. The symbol of unification is the Eucharist or Lord's Supper. Pannenberg sees that the Lord's Supper symbolizes our fellowship with God and each other, representing what it truly means to be human. In this process the Church becomes a sign of the Kingdom and whilst it is not the Kingdom or an alternate polis, it stands as a challenge to every political and judicial system that man has been a part of.[1] In this way Pannenberg believes that the Church can shine a light on secular society, but there will be very little real impact. God is present in the lives of individual believers, yet he believes the effect of this fellowship in the divine won't be experienced to any greater extent until the Kingdom comes in its fullest.

However injustice poses a deeper challenge to the Church and a call to action. Over this point Pannenberg and N.T. Wright differ significantly. Wright believes that whilst the Kingdom won't come in its fullness, each act we perform that moves towards the ideal of the Kingdom, will move into eternity. A central motif of the Church, as expounded by Lesslie Newbigin,

1.   Pannenberg, *Systematic Theology*, 51-53.

is to be a representation of God's ultimate justice. He sees that there is no separation between believing in God and following his ways in the world. Preaching the gospel and action for the Kingdom must go together and are one.[2] In missionary circles there has been much debate about the true nature of the Gospel and therefore what is demanded by it. Again this comes down to how the Kingdom is imagined and what is believed about the end times. One side of the debate believes the only valid form of mission is proclamation of the words of the gospel story. This includes creation, the story of Israel, the prophetic tradition that points to the person of Christ, his life, death and resurrection and the invitation to enter from the kingdom of darkness into the kingdom of light. Whilst these truths contain kingdom keys, to stop here limits the power of the very gospel that is proclaimed. The other side of the debate can move to the extreme also, preferring to see change in the world, often without a clear link to the Gospel story. The danger here is to forget the source of that change. The resolution of the debate was summed up well with the following story told by a missionary from the developing world. When posed with the question is real mission to give a cup of water to a thirsty person or tell them the Gospel, the simple response was, give them the water in Jesus' name. Others have been struck by the logic of the Gospel initially moving into the mission field to concentrate on the words of salvation and have found themselves starting hospitals, running schools, starting social services and being engaged in agriculture, all compelled by the Gospel's logic to bring change and social improvement.

Continuing to explore the nature of the Universal Church, Latin American theologian Gustavo Gutierrez sees the real role of the church is for liberation. This is to be worked out at three different levels. First, political, with an emphasis on oppressor and oppressed. The second level is cultural, where human history shows a progressive increase in responsibility for destiny. Thirdly, a spiritual liberation, through Christ, which restores fellowship with God. Together these parts form a salvific process which is the manifestation of the Kingdom in history, whose presence brings liberation.[3]

The concept of liberation links into the very heart of a sending God. Earlier we explored the nature of the Trinity and showed how each person in

---

2. Newbigin, *Open Secret*, 91.
3. Gustavo Gutierrez, *A Theology of Liberation*, (London: SCM, 1974), 176-177.

the Godhead has a unique role to play, yet all are linked in the missio dei (mission of God), which is essentially a mission of sending. The Father sends the Son (life, death and resurrection), the Son and the Father send the Spirit (Pentecost and the birth of the Church), and the Father, Son and Spirit send the Church into the world, to live, proclaim and work towards restoration. This understanding of mission was first articulated by Karl Barth and built upon at the 1952 Willigen Conference of the International Missionary Council.[4] The joy of this realization is profound. Mission and our work for the Kingdom does not stand on its own, but indeed it participates in the sending and self-giving activity of God.

Whilst it is the Eucharist that unites the Church to itself and to God, the Church is created for and shaped by mission, not the other way round. Mission is primarily an attribute of God. It is not that the Church has a mission of salvation, but that God does and it includes the Church.[5] The Church is an instrument for God's mission of love toward not only people, but all creation. As Abraham in Genesis 12 was blessed to be a blessing to the nations, so is the Church, which, as explored earlier, is a better way to understand the doctrine of election. Not that some are chosen and others aren't by an indiscriminate God, but that all are invited and when the blessing of the invitation is accepted, the one accepting also gets to consciously be a part of bringing the blessing of Kingdom focused change in individual lives and communities.

Evangelism and justice are two elements that lead to this change, they embody mission as "participation in God's existence in the world."[6] In this light mission can be seen as God's 'yes' to the world, and means that we need to engage in the realities of injustice, oppression, poverty, discrimination and violence. In this sense the pattern of the Church is political in as much as it is a vehicle for change. Engaging in this way provides continuity between the reign of God, the mission of the Church and God's desire for justice, peace and wholeness in society. It shows that salvation has to do with what happens to people in this world. However it does not signify that

---

4. David J. Bosch, *Transforming Mission: Paradigm Shifts in Theology of Mission,* (Maryknoll, NY: Orbis, 1991), 390.

5. J. Moltmann cited in Bosch, *Transforming Mission,* 390.

6. P. Schutz cited in Bosch, *Transforming Mission,* 10.

God's reign is now fulfilled or that the Church should once again become linked with the state.

This understanding in congruent with the picture of the Kingdom that shows God's dream for the world and implants the DNA of that dream in the world, signifying his presence. We are then able to embrace the full picture of the outworking of this dream, balancing concerns for this world and its need of salvation or restoration. Before we explore the shape of specific local expressions of the Church necessary for effective engagement, it will be helpful for us to examine the legacy that Christendom has left and its affect on the contemporary expression of church.

The Development of Christendom

From its inception in a small upper room in Jerusalem, the Church has been persecuted. Jesus' disciples and other followers were gathered after his ascension. They were scared, alone, confused. The despair of the crucifixion had turned to joy as they met and ate with Jesus post-resurrection. What followed was this amazing event as they stood and watched him disappear into the clouds. He left instructions for them to wait and pray in Jerusalem for the Holy Spirit. As they were gathered doing just that, they suddenly experienced what felt like wind and earthquake and saw tongues of fire reaching out to touch those gathered. Those praying were not hurt, but were given the ability to speak in different languages. Jerusalem has always been a multi-cultural city and as such there were devout Jews from around the known world staying there. The noise of the wind caused a crowd to gather who stood in amazement as they heard the story about Jesus in their own language. Some thought the Apostles were drunk, others believed, and that day about three thousand people became followers of Jesus, joining what would become known as the Church. You can read the full story of the birth of the Church in Acts 2.

Initially the Church was seen as a Jewish sect, but was soon ejected from Judaism and as persecution grew the believers scattered, taking the gospel with them. Those remaining in Jerusalem met secretly in houses and catacombs. Over time as the numbers in the Church grew, all over the known world, it became a threat to the Emperor cult. The Roman Empire was a blessing and a curse to the Church. They had provided roads and infrastructure to enable effective trade across the expansive empire, making it easy to travel and share the good news. However, at the same time the

Emperor saw himself as a god and there was to be no worship of any other god but him. Of course people following Jesus did not want to bow down to anyone but God. This led many to be punished in some of the most horrific ways, including being taken to the Colosseum and ripped apart by gladiators or lions.

It was into this environment that Constantine became emperor in early 300s CE. Originally he followed the Emperor Cult and persecuted any religion, including the Followers of the Way as the Christians came to be known. Then in around 311CE he changed his mind. Some scholars believe he became a Christian, while others question his motives. However, he signed a declaration which led the way for the toleration of Christianity. This was ratified two years later in the Edict of Milan signed both by Constantine who ruled in the west of the empire, and Licinius who ruled in the East. The edict essentially granted an indulgence for Christians to be able to pray and worship in safety. In the following years Constantine issued further edicts that brought about the restoration of confiscated property, saw the subsidizing of the Church by the state, exempted the clergy from public service, banned soothsaying, and established Sunday as a day of rest and worship. By 325CE, Constantine had also assumed a position of theological leadership at the Council of Nicaea. This all despite the number of Christians being only a tenth of the population of the Roman Empire.[7]

Between 313CE and the eleventh century the Roman Empire underwent significant transformation. The empire was divided into East and West. The Western sphere centred in Ravenna, whilst by 330CE Constantine had moved the Eastern centre to Byzantium, changing its name to Constantinople (City of Constantine). This was a strategic move that strengthened the Eastern part of the Empire from attack and recognized the Eastern roots of Christianity.[8] After constant attacks Constantinople finally fell in 476CE to the Germanic king, Odoacer. Roman authority also completely collapsed in the West, and became a patchwork of Germanic kingdoms. However, the city of Rome under the guidance of the Catholic Church became a centre of learning. Throughout the sixth century, the Eastern part of the old empire was in constant conflict, firstly with the Persians and then the rise of Islamic Caliphate. In the West, because of the

---

7. Earl E. Cairns, *Christianity Through The Centuries*, (Grand Rapids, MI: Zondervan, 1978), 134-135.

8. Bruce L. Shelley, *Church History in Plain Language*, (Dallas, TX: Word, 1995), 95.

vacuum left by the Empire's collapse, the beginnings of the feudal system emerged, in the form of localized hierarchies. These were based on the bond of the common people to the land on which they worked. Through this system new princes and kings arose of which the greatest was the Frank ruler Charlemagne.[9] In 800CE he was crowned Emperor of the Romans.[10] This saw the beginning of the Germanic Roman Empire, also known as the Holy Roman Empire or See. Through a military relationship with the Papacy, forged by his grandfather and father, Charlemagne protected Pope Leo III from being mutinied. The Pope had been accused amongst other things of perjury and adultery. By way of peacemaking Charlemagne presided over a large assembly of bishops, nobles, diplomats and rebels. At the end of the assembly Pope Leo III took an oath purging himself of these accusations. In return a couple of days later the Pope crowned Charlemagne Emperor, restoring the Christian Roman Empire. In this way the Christian concept of a universal, Catholic Church was grafted onto the traditional Roman view of Empire, and Christendom was created.

By the eleventh century Christianity was fully grown and in control of the culture. By the Middle Ages there was institutional interdependence between the pope and the ruler of the Holy Roman See.[11] Even when there were disputes between the two rulers, they operated within the framework of Christendom or the corpus Christianum. During this period there was the rise of nation states within Western Europe, including the Vikings settling in Britain, Ireland and France; the Kingdom of Hungary; and the Normans in Southern Italy. Each of these states were under the influence of the Church.[12]

As the reformation surfaced, it dealt a severe blow to this symbiotic relationship. The Church in the West was no longer one, however the idea of Christendom remained in tact. That is, the Church was enmeshed with the state in the distribution of power. In each European country the

---

9. Carl Stephenson and Bryce Lyon, ed., *Mediaeval History: Europe from the Second to Sixteenth Century,* (New York, NY: Harper and Row, 1951), 150-151.
After various military marks and marches, Charlemagne's territory extended in the East from the Baltic Seas to the head of the Adriatic, in the South to Croatia and Pannonia and the North to Moravia and Bohemia.

10. Shelley, *Church History in Plain Language,* 173-174.

11. Frost and Hirsch, *The Shaping of Things to Come,* 8.

12. Shelley, *Church History in Plain Language,* 184.

Church developed into a state church. At this point in time it was difficult to differentiate between political, cultural and religious elements and activities.[13]

Just as a side note, this difficulty in differentiating the different motivations of any particular action of the state or indeed cultural response to issues can inform our response to terrorism that takes place in the name of Islam. I am by no means an expert in Middle Eastern affairs. However, I suspect Islam as a religion, in being tied to nation states as Christianity was and still is in some parts of the world, has taken on cultural and political expressions not true to its original motivations. I'm writing in the aftermath of attacks in Brussels, with some academic analysts believing that radicalization of minorities within Belgium due to social exclusion could be a significant factor in these events.[14] So whilst they might be motivated by a group such as ISIS they gain traction in a country like Belgium due to a response to cultural situations.

The Effects of Christendom

To understand the effect of this period of history on the Church we need to make brief comparisons with what went before. Hirsch and Frost argue that the Church pre 313CE was characterized by its persecuted and underground nature. It was de-centralized and didn't have any buildings. The leadership was holistic and employed the gifts of apostle, prophet, evangelist, pastor and teacher. A central feature of the gathered community was communion in the form of a sacralized community meal. The Church identified itself as missionary in nature and incarnational in relationship. After the Edict of Milan and the eventual marrying of church and state, buildings became central to the understanding and experience of Church. There was a very definite structural hierarchy. The pastor/teacher became the predominant gift mix of the leadership of the Church. Grace was determined by and delivered through the institutionalized sacraments.[15]

---

13. Bosch, *Transforming Mission,* 275.

14. Martin Conway, "The Bitter Fruits of Alienation: Belgium's Struggle is the Problem of Our Age," *The Conversation,* 24 March, 2016, accessed 24 March, 2016, http://theconversation.com/the-bitter-fruits-of-alienation-belgiums-struggle-is-the-problem-of-our-age-56758.

15. Frost and Hirsch, *The Shaping of Things to Come,* 9.

Through the Enlightenment period (which we will explore in greater detail in the next chapter), the Church began to lose its influence on society. Today in the West we live largely in a post-Christian, post-Christendom society. However the Church continues to largely view the world through a Christendom mindset, quite often operating with an air of entitlement. When Christendom was at its height, the Church controlled the values of society, owned a lot of property and closely influenced the politics of the day, with bishops being regular guests in the court of the kings. Subconsciously in the Church's psyche is the belief that it should still have that influence.

For a time I was part of a movement that stated it wanted to help the Church regain its place in the centre of the community. A noble goal, that longs for the days where the church had a significant influence in the life of the village. I have only realized through this period of reflection that the statement is in fact linked closely to regaining a sense of Christendom. I don't think the leaders of the movement necessarily saw this as a political move. However, it demonstrates how subtly Christendom can still affect the missional imagination.

Christendom has also left a legacy in the Church of wanting power, buildings and wealth. The little fellowship that my parents attend recently bought a building in their seaside town. A rumour was surfacing that their long term meeting place was up for development. I'm not sure of all the reasons they decided to buy, but the point is, the desire to do so was obviously present. Whilst there is nothing wrong with a church having a building, it can become its focus. When Amy and I were first married we attended the church where she grew up, a Baptist church situated in a seaside suburb of Adelaide. Over the time we were there as a couple the church began to grow and decided it needed to extend, so a building program was put together as well as an appeal for funds. Eventually the building was renovated with the outcome being a new auditorium and more spaces for group activities. The mayor of the municipality opened the new building with a challenge to the church. The core question he left with the church was, now that you have this bright shiny new building, what are you going to do with it? Is it just going to be for in-house use or is it something that will benefit the whole community?

Many mainline denominations still own a lot of property, with the Catholic Church being one of the largest landowners in the world.[16] Again this is a legacy from Christendom where the church, community and political structure were closely linked. Power or influence also continues to be a key driver in some parts of the Church. This can lead to an almost bullying approach to social and moral issues, seen most recently in some of the debates around same sex attraction and in the Australian parliament over the Safe Schools program. The approach taken by some parts of the Church to the public debate suggests a worldview that says if don't see the issue in the same way we do then you are wrong. The moral high ground is always being presumed. It could be argued that some on the conservative side of the debate forget the biblical call to justice, mercy and compassion in favour of a moralistic approach, based on Christendom entitlement.

When Christendom was at its height the morals of the Church were the morals of the society, the case is not the same today. However that does not mean that as the Church we can force our beliefs on others and expect them to comply. Because of our Christendom based entitlement we have failed to read our current culture correctly and contextualize our understanding of the gospel and its application. This has led to completely different understandings of the world and, for a raft of reasons, the Church being locked out of the public debate. Some would blame the secularization of our culture, liberalism and its child, individualism. Whilst these are significant factors to be aware of, it is a failure of the Church to connect effectively with a changing world, and a changing status within that world. If these things are taken into account it is entirely plausible that the Church can have a positive voice in the public debate towards a better world.

To round off this discussion on Christendom it will be helpful for us to look with fresh eyes at where God is present in our culture and how the Church can engage with what he is doing.

Stamps of the Divine in Our Culture

The political situation for asylum seekers in Australia is not good. In an effort to 'turn back the boats' the government has decided that the majority of asylum seekers and refugees that attempt to arrive by boat will either be

---

16. Thornton McEnery, "World's 15 Biggest Landowners, " Business Insider Australia, last updated 19 March, 2016, accessed March 24 2016, http://www.businessinsider.com.au/worlds-biggest-landowners-2011-3?r=US&IR=T#3-pope-benedict-13.

turned around and sent back to the port where the boat originated from or sent to Manus or Nauru Islands. There have been agreements made with the governments of these island nations, with detention centres being established and the opportunity for people to settle in these countries. Whilst on the outset this sounds like a workable solution, in reality the Australian government is being incredibly cruel, stating that asylum seekers or refugees that attempt to enter the country this way will never be allowed to settle in this country. People, including children, are being held indefinitely in these isolated communities, left with no certainty and no hope about their future. Unintentionally perhaps, the engine room for these decisions and actions is formed by a connection between the government and media, fuelling the fear of the average Aussie towards people who are different. The result is young children harming themselves due to depression and other illnesses and adults committing suicide. I have been dismayed when reading comments in newspapers and listening to callers to the shock jocks saying that these people deserve what they get and we need to look after our own first.

Whilst this sounds like a culture devoid of the divine, there are some alternate voices gaining traction in the community. *Love Makes A Way,* started by Jarrod McKenna, have been joining their voice with other Christian leaders, conducting sit-ins and other advocacy, asking for all children to be released from detention centres. The divine value of compassion, particularly for the poor and destitute, is broader in the community than those with a Christian faith. In February 2016 a Brisbane hospital refused to release a child who with her mother had been brought from Nauru due to accidental burns sustained in the detention centre. A spokesperson from the Lady Cilento Children's Hospital said, "All decisions relating to a patient's treatment and discharge are made by qualified clinical staff, based on a thorough assessment of the individual patient's clinical condition and circumstances, and with the goal of delivering the best outcome." The spokesperson also commented "(she) will only be discharged once a suitable home environment is identified."[17]

---

17. Nicole Hasham, "Hospital refused to discharge asylum seeker toddler to prevent return to Nauru," *Sydney Morning Herald*, 13 February, 2016, accessed March 31 2016, http://www. smh.com.au/national/nauru-baby-being-kept-by-brisbane-hospital-20160212-gmt3dg. html.

Connected to this wave of compassion was talk of sending a further two hundred and sixty-seven asylum seekers back to Nauru, including thirty-seven children. They had been allowed to come to Australia for medical concerns, including terminal cancer. The government wanted to send many back to the detention centre. This came to prominence and there was a 'let them stay' backlash, with spontaneous rallies being organized. In addition, the Premier of Victoria wrote a letter to the Prime Minister stating that Victoria would take all two hundred and sixty-seven and work to house and support them. Other premiers followed suit. There were also a number of church leaders who invoked the ancient rite of sanctuary.[18] It is still not clear if this would have stood up legally. However, the fact remains that many in the Australian community responded with compassion and generosity, both hallmarks of the divine. The Church responded in such a way that it was a core proponent of mercy and compassion in the greater society.

Other stamps of the divine include acts of kindness. I wonder how many little acts of kindness come your way everyday or even ones you perform without thinking about them. Someone holds a door for you, or in our building waits for you before closing the lift doors. Or perhaps a random person lets you into the flow of traffic, or offers an elderly person a seat on public transport. I witnessed a quite astounding act of kindness on a tram. One particularly warm morning, the tram I was on, despite it being fairly new and packing what I suspect was a good cooling system, was incredibly stuffy. I was sweating from rushing for the tram and I could see others visibly uncomfortable with the pack of people and the atmosphere in the tram. A passenger became ill and in fact fainted. I saw this happen and was about to move towards them when others came to the assistance. Someone helped lower the person to the floor and others, despite the crowded environment made room. The passenger came around fairly quickly. It was at the next stop that I was truly amazed. Another passenger, a complete stranger to the person needing assistance, got off at the stop and waited with them until further help arrived. It is acts like these that begin to point to a divine reality in our world.

---

18. Ben Doherty, "Let them stay: Backlash in Australia against plans to send asylum seekers to detention camps," *The Guardian*, 10 February, 2016, accessed March 31, 2016, http://www.theguardian.com/australia-news/2016/feb/10/let-them-stay-australia-backlash-267-asylum-seekers-island-detention-camps.

Of course big and small acts of kindness happen every day, from a smile, which can change someone's day to the offer of a house, which can change their life. Neal, who works serving the homeless and marginalized in the Yarra Ranges was recently the recipient of kindness. He and his family needed to move house due to the landlord redeveloping the property. Being on a small income with a wife and three children did not make the search for a house in the area easy. A partner of the work lives on a property owned by another organization. On a visit to the property Neal saw vacant houses and sent up a prayer of wonder, feeling it would be great to be able to live on the property. When he caught up with the partner she said she had been talking with the managers of the property and they wanted to offer him and his family a place to live with affordable rent and the benefits that come with being able to mix with others in a community-like environment.

Nature, even in our built up urban environments, is another stamp of the divine in our society. Each morning I take our little dog for a walk, through the housing reserve on which we live. There is one particular point where I can't help but admire the trees as the morning light shimmers on the leaves. Every time I see it, I'm reminded that God is present in every situation.

God is even present in suffering. I have recently experienced a couple of operations, the first and hopefully the last for a long time. In each experience I was surrounded by excellent doctors and, particularly, nurses who respected my dignity and cared for every need I had. During my first stay in hospital my recovery was slow and I was quite sick. I remember reflecting afterwards with my spiritual director, saying I felt the absence of God. We reflected on the excellent care I received and this helped me see the medical profession (and my wife Amy) as the hands and feet of God, caring and providing for me.

God is present everywhere his values are present, including in the work of local councils. During 2015 I was part of consultations with Wyndham City Council. My role was to facilitate four consultations with different communities within the municipality. The aim was to bring out the strengths of these communities and explore ways they could be built upon. As the individual workshops gathered momentum it was heartening to witness people with a desire to see their communities flourish, thinking creatively about how this could happen. These kinds of processes are always fraught with danger, most significantly the time lag between consultation and action. However with good communication, energy can be maintained and the community galvanized into action for its own future. We will explore this later in the book.

There are plenty more examples of where God is present in our society, both working through the church and outside it. He is working on his blueprint for the Kingdom in the world now. The invitation is for us to join with him. In the following chapter we will explore the shape of individual faith communities needed to fully join with God on his task.

Reflection Questions

1. Have you seen God as an exclusivist or inclusivist? How does being blessed to be a blessing to others change your perception of those around you and your mission?

2. How does the unity of the Church expressed through the Lord's Supper or Eucharist impact on how you might partner with other churches in your community?

3. How have the churches you have been, or are, connected with been affected by Christendom? What remedies are there for this?

4. Some Christians seem to like painting the world in a negative light, however if the Kingdom of God is present with us now then so are the effects of that. Were have you seen stamps of the divine in your culture/community/city?

Chapter 5. - The Shape of the Gathered Community

The church exists primarily for two closely correlated purposes: to worship God and work for his kingdom in the world... The church also exists for a third purpose, which serves the other two: to encourage one another, to build one another up in faith, to pray with and for one another, to learn from one another and teach one another, and to set one another examples to follow, challenges to take up, and urgent tasks to perform. This is all part of what is known loosely as fellowship.

N.T. Wright

As well as having a universal element, the church also has a particular shape or footprint in a local community. The specifics of any local shape can be as numerous as the number of churches. However, to be effective in the world there are some broad brushstroke values and perspective that will guide a local expression.

As a gathered community the church is to reflect the Trinitarian nature of the Kingdom; that is, recognizing the presence of the Father, Son and Holy Spirit and letting each person of the Trinity have the space for their unique focus to be present. To be authentic the church also needs to recognize its eschatological ontology; that is, it's very being, the essence of who the church is, originated from God's ultimate future. This future broke into our world through Jesus' death on the cross and his resurrection, making it possible for God's Kingdom (his eschatological future) to dwell with us and have real impact in the world now.

These two realities set up a tension between the inner workings of any local congregation and the outworking of mission in the world. In many churches there is a dichotomy between these two tensions, with one being clearly demonstrated as more important than the other. However if a community is to be holistic it needs to recognize that both elements of Trinity and eschatological ontology need to be held together for the effective outworking of the Gospel.

These realities point to a number of essential elements that shape the inner working of the church or community. Framing all of these aspects is the essential element of love. In John 13:35 Jesus clearly states that those who aren't a part of any church will be drawn by the love evident between the believers. This begs a couple of questions; firstly, do we love each other? Secondly, if we do love each other, how do people get to see that love? Love was a key hallmark for believers in the early church, they regularly held what was called agape or love feasts where typically a house church would gather and eat together. The book of Acts bears witness that their love for each other went further than this, with people selling all they had in order to share what they needed. Together as a fellowship, they were seen to have everything in common.

What difference would it make to our work and ministry if we began to shape it around love or, you might like to say, relationships or people? Most claim that their ministry is centred in just that, and for all intents and purposes the motivations of our work is good. However we often fail to ask: what is love and what expression does that need to take? We will explore this further in subsequent chapters. For now though, the focus is on our love for each other. If you are part of a church, when you think about the relationships in your church what words come to mind? If you are involved in ministries that, for example, feed the poor or provide housing or support in some way, how does your team relate? The same questions can be asked of people working in social services and local councils: what are the relationships like between the people in your organization? How are they modelling wholeness to the people they work with? I suspect it is similar in other cultures, but Aussies are particularly defensive about being told what to do. They need to see it and preferably experience a different way in order to begin to want to move down that path.

When I was working with Fusion, a Christian youth and community organization, we used to run community festivals. Quite often this was done in partnership with local churches. One of the questions we asked in our teaching and would remind ourselves was when does the festival start? Seems a simple question to answer -whatever time is on the flyer. However it wasn't as easy as that. The festival really got underway as soon as the team started arriving on the ground to set up. Right from the outset of the day we needed to be practising amongst one another the hospitality that others would receive as they waited in line for a sausage. The love and gentleness experienced by those getting their face painted needed to be evidenced between each other as the tents were erected. The welcome that would be given from the stage and through the giant interactive games needed to be offered to each team member as they arrived to play their part.

The process of creating an open environment as described above challenges us in a couple of ways. First, the love experienced in a church congregation can be cliquey and conditional, rather than open and boundless, accepting and including of the stranger. Have you ever gone to a new church or been visiting for a day and had no one talk with you? Instead you stood there watching as others engaged in conversation and began to feel a bit lost, sneaking out the door, hoping not to be noticed. Yes, it has happened to me! The kind of love that is described in the festival environment is the love that, yes, sustains each other but is also open to welcome others. Demonstrating this sort of love and acceptance is even harder for those in the social services and local council. However even with professional distance it is not impossible to be genuine, warm, other person-focused and so on. The basis for much of this comes from the internal dynamic of the team or organization.

The second challenge the type of love demonstrated in a festival lays before us is how we view those we are seeking to help. The festival environment can best be described as an open crowd, where all are seen and valued and can make a contribution. A festival of this sort is working best when you can't tell the difference between the team and the participants. Sound chaotic? It can be. However, the results are startling as people begin to participate. They become open to one another and deep and significant conversations evolve between strangers or those that hardly know each other. The usual rituals of conversation and reservation seem to be leapt over and relationships evolve quite quickly. Whilst not every environment is a festival environment, they can be open and inclusive if those we are seeking to serve feel valued, respected and given the opportunity to contribute.

I was recently asked by a denomination in Sydney to design an evaluation process for their care arm. *Careworks* is essentially a partnership between the work of individual churches in the community and the denomination. Encouragingly, they are working on establishing cohesive structures and best practice across the movement. One of the key factors we discussed in the evaluation process and subsequent training was the view people running programs held of those they are seeking to help. We asked the specific question: is there room for genuine (not tokenistic) contribution?

An organization that provides space for contribution is *Servants Community Housing* based in Hawthorn, one of Melbourne's leafy inner city suburbs. Servants is a ministry housing around ninety people, most suffering with some kind of mental illness. It started in the mid-1980s born out of the *Radical Discipleship* movement of the 1970s and growing as a missional expression of the community generated at the Hawthorn West Baptist Church. Through the houses an environment of deep hospitality is established where residents feel they belong just as they are. This sense of welcome, value and place combines to create a safe atmosphere where people are freed to explore who they really are. Matt, the CEO, tells the story of Don:

> When Don came to Servants he was basically a cave man who for five years would not look at himself in the mirror. He was estranged from his family and for all intents and purposes a recluse. Servants gave him a small, clean room and let the environment of the community soak into him. After a time, Don began to come out of his shell. He has now spoken about Servants at a book launch and other events and has recently gone to America to visit his family.

Whilst not actively seeking this kind of contribution or personal transformation, Servants, through its culture based on the three core values of respect, dignity and hope, provides the opportunity for participant-led contribution; be it as simple as setting the table or tending the garden, being part of a social enterprise or representing the organization at an event.

So what are the essential values and perspective (shape) necessary for a church to emulate this sort of welcome? I am not so interested in exploring what a service might look like or even the inner mechanics of a particular church. I'm more interested in the attitudes and perspectives that we hold as individuals that go towards making up our inner and outer expression as a community of faith.

Sacramental and Unifying Nature of the Church

To round off our conversation on the universal Church it is helpful for each local expression to understand that it is part of the whole. Together we live under what Alan Hirsch in *The Forgotten Ways* refers to as a Christologically redefined shema. In Deuteronomy 6:4 God makes a claim over his people. YWHW is to be Israel's God and he is one. This is followed by a command that the people are to love the God who is one with all their heart, soul and strength. This can be seen as God lifting his people out of a polytheistic milieu towards monotheism. In this the command to love is a call to covenant loyalty, and a dethronement of all other gods.[1] The sense of God's oneness and his call to loyalty continues in the New Testament. Matthew 6:33 calls God's followers to seek his Kingdom first above everything else. In turn, because we define our relationship with God through Jesus, we can understand our belief as Christocentric monotheism.[2] The preceding verses talk in black and white terms about those who don't follow being concerned about what they will eat, drink and wear; in fact they will be consumed by these worries.

In our consumer driven society it is easy to see how material goods and even the necessities can become gods of our preoccupation. When I was engaged to marry Amy, we were both quite young and had a number of well meaning people from our church come and talk with us about how it would be better for us to finish study, build a solid financial base and then get married. Now I'm not saying that our motives in getting married were all about following God into some bright future, we were young and we wanted to get on with the adventure, however somewhere in those mixed emotions and feelings we had the sense that there was more to life than studying just to get a job, earning money to buy a car, saving for a house and so on. From the outset our life together has been about being as faithful to God as we know how. This has not been a simple journey but it has been our faltering attempt to follow Jesus' call to put God's Kingdom first. This understanding is the roots referred to in radical discipleship, the core understanding of the centrality of God in every decision and in every aspect of our world. Putting God's Kingdom first and all that goes with that action is what is meant to set the people of God apart. Unfortunately what tends to set us apart currently is a hypocritical narrow moralism, that sees some protesting loudly about same sex marriage and abortion, whilst the gap between rich and poor increase, communities break down, homelessness and familylessness continue to rise and key leaders brush paedophilia under the carpet.

Alternatively radical discipleship seeks to hold the tension between righteousness and justice, recognizing that there are shades of grey and that we should be, first and foremost, promoting God's love for the world

1.　Alan Hirsch, *The Forgotten Ways: Reactivating the Missional Church,* (Grand Rapids, MI: Brazos, 2006), 89.

2.　Hirsch, *The Forgotten Ways,* 93.

and his desire for it to reflect the reality of his Kingdom's presence. The shema, reinforced by Jesus (Mark 12:30-31) is a helpful starting point in discovering the Church's shape in the world as God's people. It is God's covenant claim and is the unshakable centre of creed and confession. The Church's commitment to the person of Christ shapes not only our understanding of who we are, but our actions in the world as his body.

Because of the unique relationship between the gathered ecclesia and the one in whose name we gather, the inner working of the community is by nature sacramental. The gathering exhibits the incarnation of divine activity within human activity.[3] As Paul points out in Ephesians, there is one lord, one faith, one baptism (Eph 4:4-5). As the gathered community lives in the reality of this, we realize there is a fundamental commonality in ecclesial practices. In each culture the outworking of the practices may be different. However, wherever baptism is practised it is a gateway into God's new creation, inaugurated in the resurrection of Jesus. As explored earlier, the celebration of the Eucharist is to remind us of our unity as the people who share in the suffering and victory of Christ. From an outward or missional perspective it also reminds us that we are to be communities of gratitude and generosity, in solidarity with the hungry, dispossessed and marginalized.[4] These elements of ecclesial life and those we are about to explore are universal because they are derived from the witness of Scripture, which is based in the life and ministry of Jesus. However each will need to be interpreted by the unique cultural settings that the community of faith finds itself in.

Buildings and Geography

The concept of place and geographic community are the subject of many conversations both inside and external to the church. Local councils are seeing the importance of a neighbourhood approach to building community, where they create a hub with various activities and learning opportunities for the immediate area. These may include a childcare facility or a kindergarten as well as physical space for groups to meet. Wyndham City Council in the West of Melbourne have set up a number of these hubs, some even co-locating with a library or youth services.

---

3.   Darrell L. Guder, ed., *Missional Church: A Vision for the Sending of the Church in North America*, (Grand Rapids, MI: Eerdmans, 1989), 180.

4.   Guder ed., *Missional Church*, 181-182.

The hub concept is not that different to the parish model for churches, where a church was built to be the hub or one of the key gathering places for the community. Some churches are again looking at this concept, though not through Christendom eyes as would have once been the case, but seeing buildings as an opportunity to connect with the community. Liberation Theology, which we will look at in greater depth later, also inspired the development of community halls as opposed to cathedrals. These community spaces were used to train locals in many and varied skills, creating an opportunity for the community to come together and raise its voice against oppression.

Buildings can also be seen as a negative. A quote attributed to Winston Churchill spells out the dangers of becoming too focused on a structure: 'we build our buildings and then our buildings build us.' He is referring to the tendency for an organization to be shaped by the space it inhabits. Whilst churches can use their buildings as community facilities they can also be a contributing factor to insularity. Some church buildings even begin to feel like the clubhouse, with arguments over the colour of the carpets or the layout of the kitchen taking precious energy and focus away from the church's mission. Buildings can also be a left-over from Christendom, displaying the power and wealth of the church to a community that is suspicious about its intentions.

However because of the commitment to the theology of new creation, geography and buildings still have a place in the missional expression of the church. By new creation I mean recognizing that Jesus' resurrection ushered in the possibility for all of creation to be renewed. This includes humankind. Jesus is the first fruit of this new creation, inviting us to join him in the work of renewal. If we do away with buildings totally, we fall prone to a dualism that negates God's investment of the future in the present. God's plan encompasses a total renewal of all creation but in the meantime, because of the presence of the Kingdom, he is already engaged in the work of renewing. So perhaps the question becomes, how can we redeem the buildings used by churches and even redeem communities or neighbourhoods to be part of the renewed creation?

Going further down this path, buildings can create an opportunity for what the Celtics call thin space, where the curtain separating heaven and earth becomes almost transparent.[5] This is commonly understood to happen during worship, but it is possible to see any experience that gives opportunity for God to be at work in the world as thin space. Spaces where God is particularly present and active can occur in a café, a lounge-room or even in a park. They could even take place in a festival. However, spaces dedicated to worship can help people make the connection between the spiritual and the material, enabling a more holistic approach to life and faith. There is plenty of room for the creative engagement with space that further fosters these connections.

If as the Church we are to embrace our mission to a world of space, time and matter we can't ignore or marginalize that world. Rather, we need to redeem it, explaining through action and word that God is the God of all that we see and experience around us.[6] This includes what happens in our local area. In so many ways our world has become de-centralized, this is also true for the community. We no longer live and work in a village, but rather tend to travel long distances from our home in the outer suburbs to work in the CBD. These dual lives can cause problems.

During my time living and ministering in Pakenham, I had the honour of being invited to be part of the welfare committee at the Consolidated Primary School. We met every week to explore the wellbeing of students at the rather large and continuing to grow primary school. We would often talk about different programs and how they could be integrated into the teaching life of the school. One conversation was particularly fascinating, as we named the disconnect between some parents and their children. Pakenham is what is known as a dormitory suburb, where many people leave the community everyday to travel up to sixty kilometres to go to work. It is also a fairly young suburb with many new housing estates taking up the land that used to be paddocks. This means that as families move into the community, recreation and even shopping can continue to take place in old networks. However, their children at the Consolidated Primary School were being encouraged to get to know their community and its history, in effect to form a bond with their space. Parents with lives elsewhere, children establishing connection, meaning and even roots in the new community - the playing field was set up for confusion and cognitive

---

5. Wright, *Surprised by Hope*, 270-271.

6. Wright, *Surprised by Hope*, 276.

dissonance, the effect of this at times becoming palpable in the playground through children acting out aggressively.

All this to say that place matters. My family and I often remark to others that our community of Fitzroy has a village feel about it. Being inner city, there is a wide diversity of people who call the community home. However, you don't have to look too far for someone who is willing to stop and have a chat over washing at the launderette, travelling between floors in the lift or on the reserve with the dogs. It seems easier to share common bonds and experience life in some form of connection.

As we think about buildings and place the challenge for the Church is to have a theology that allows and takes into account the materiality of this world and recognizes that God wants to redeem it. This theology needs to include an understanding of the importance of place for the human psyche. A theology of this nature puts a call out to people of faith to once again inhabit a neighbourhood, be present in it and work to be aware of what God's grace looks like for the people of that community. The Benedictines, a Catholic order, affirm the importance of place and in fact hold stability as a high value and as such are committed to living in the one place. Noel Castellanos, CEO of Christian Community Development Association, believes that to be effective in a community people need to commit at least fifteen years to living and working in that space.[7] Having had a ministry in many different places around Australia I find this thinking very challenging, yet see the importance of stability and long term commitment if our work is to be truly incarnational.

Prayer

A common question asked by pastors, Christian counsellors and spiritual directors of people who come to them in distress or for some issue relating to their discipleship is, how's your prayer life? Another way of asking the question is, how is your relationship with God? These are such fundamental questions because they go to the heart of any motivation for the Christian life or missional engagement with local communities. The question signals a dependence that for many of us we resist quite strongly, leading to a dry religiosity or, even more subtly, a feeling that we need to earn our place with God.

---

7. Christian Community Development Association, www.ccda.org.

Personally, over the last couple of years my prayer life has changed dramatically. Not least due to my spiritual director who works in a completely different stream of Christianity than I had experienced. I first started seeing Rob due to a nagging restlessness that there was more to experience in my spiritual life. During the previous couple of years there had been a fair bit of personal and professional upheaval that had left me questioning God's goodness and his care of me. When I first started seeing Rob I would have described myself as a recovering workaholic. I'm not sure how far the recovery had actually gotten, as I remember sessions where I would debrief my busyness and my attempts to 'save' the world, as well as the conflict I was experiencing on that journey. Looking back, these must have caused Rob some amusement. Without me knowing it, he was really listening to a burnt-out activist.

I slowly became aware of my frenetic activities and the effect they were having on my health, my sense of wellbeing and my relationships, particularly those closest to me. You know that feeling where you are moving quickly, doing lots of things, but not really getting anywhere? There was lots of surface energy, like a car with damaged pistons. The engine can rev quite hard but the power is not getting to the wheels and so there isn't much forward momentum. In hindsight it was as if the work I was doing was not coming from all of me. I had always felt that I had a close relationship with God (predominantly Father and Son, with occasional connection to the Spirit). I would journal most days and used to be inspired by Scripture, but these practices began to fall short and I found myself feeling dry and worn out.

Under Rob's guidance (and with the support of other mentors) I began to explore different understandings of myself, my journey, God and what lay ahead. A core change that probably set many other changes in motion was a change in my understanding of how guidance worked. I used to look externally for God's leading, a sign in Scripture, a response to a need, the desire for adventure and what looked like the next step, and of course the thoughts of other people. One day this understanding of guidance shifted and I found myself looking internally. This is not to be mistaken with introspection, however guidance became more of a journey to discover my authentic self, with the 'what can I do?' question coming out of that.

A core part of this journey has been engagement with contemplative prayer. Whilst initially this felt like a reduction in intimacy as it was a change of habit, from writing to simply experiencing, it has been central in discovering a deeper intimacy and connection. In turn these things are leading slowly to changing perspectives of myself, my role in the world and how I view others. I still have a long way to go and there are hiccups and more perspectives yet to change, but I can see already how I am bringing more of myself, my true character to what I am doing.

This is also true of the Church. If it is to reflect its true nature as the people of God it needs to be a praying church. Prayer is the beginning of the recognition that there is a power and person beyond us. N.T. Wright picks up on the essential elements of prayer, naming them as mysticism and petition. Mysticism coming out of a long and ancient tradition of desert mystics and others, opens us to the beauty of the world and its createdness, drawing us into a deeper and more intimate relationship with the creator. Have you ever stopped and admired the beauty of a sunrise or a sunset, the different colours in the sky, how the light interacts with the environment? Or perhaps you've watched a bird playing. When I was young I remember walking through a park and being amazed at a flock of swallows playing in an old pipe. They would cheekily fly through it over and over again, faster each time, chirping all the while, tempting others to join them. Taking the time to see creation is a form of mystic practice, where we can recognize and experience oneness with the creator.

The second element of prayer is petition. Confession time: I have never really been good at praying for others. When asked, of course I do, and when I've had pastoral responsibility for others I have sought to bring them before God. Some people are fantastic list pray-ers, they can spend hours bringing other people before God asking for his mercy and justice. Both forms of prayer can be found in ancient pagan traditions, with one key difference. The pagan communities were unable to overcome fear of the deities. An individual would petition a particular god for favours or protection, only to live in fear that someone who had sacrificed more would get the blessing.[8]

Wright goes on to explain that the balance of mysticism and petition is evident in the spirituality of God's people Israel as portrayed in the Hebrew Scriptures (Old Testament). Through the Psalms and other passages we can see their marveling at creation, the wonder of its vastness and the place

---

8.   Wright, *Surprised by Hope*, 289-290.

of humans in that vastness. In the same way, through this marveling they were drawn into an intimate relationship with the creator of the vastness. There were other times in the Psalms, Lamentations and elsewhere where they petitioned the creator. This continued even when he appeared distant. They would remind him of his personal promises. At times they would even come to the sorrowful realization of the need to leave their petitions at God's door.[9] Through this very short look at biblical prayer we can see elements of transcendence (recognition of the need to be connected to something/someone beyond humanity), intimacy (that it's possible to be in a deep loving relationship with that person), celebration (that we can revel in God's goodness through creation, presence and blessing), and covenant (that these connections don't happen randomly but are part of an agreement between God and his people).

To be effective in the world the Church's spirituality needs to reflect these elements. Transcendence will allow connection with a bigger dream and the possibility of a better world. Realizing God's total otherness shows that the world we are working for now, actually comes from somewhere beyond us, but breaks into our time and space, through the benevolence of a creator who not only created in the first place but is concerned with re-creation and invites us to be part of the journey. This sets the stage and the motivation for our own sacrifice.

Intimacy with God - I am learning again how sweet this is, and how he pursues us and longs for us to develop this depth of connection with him. God's desire for intimacy shows that he is not a hard taskmaster, but desires first and foremost to truly meet with us, for us to be present with him. Every act of service, whether in or outside of the church, needs to stem from this realization and experience. If it doesn't we are in danger of seeking and working towards our picture of a better world. This will inevitably cause a skewed view of those we are trying to help and our role as helpers. Later we will discuss the contemporary debate between welfare and community development. It is possible for our best intentions to become toxic. Without a growing intimacy our work will have a brittle quality about it and lack the wholeness that grace offers. Intimacy also allows us the opportunity on a personal and corporate level to explore who we are or who we have been created to be and adjust our service and sacrifice to be expressions of this ontology, rather than trying to fit into a world of 'should's.

---

9. Wright, *Surprised by Hope*, 290.

A third characteristic of the Church's prayer is celebration; recognizing that we are people who embody the goodness, presence and blessing of God. The Church is often seen as austere or at the very best removed from the common experience. Rather, a grounded or earthly spirituality allows for true celebration. This can be and is expressed in many of our gatherings, with some denominations doing better than others at living celebration. This is commonly referred to as praise. However celebration can take many forms. I was part of a movement known as Awakening 2000. The centrepiece of the movement was an annual Easter Sunday March taking place in most capital cities around Australia. This was an opportunity for the churches to come together in the city and celebrate and proclaim together publicly that Jesus is risen and a new day has dawned. The marchers were all dressed colourfully, carrying balloons that echoed the reason for the celebration. They would quite often converge from different corners of the city to some central point, where a festival would continue the celebrations. This was always covered by the media, offering an alternative to rather stiff and staunch Easter services. Generally, the Australian culture is not good at meaningful celebration, however this is something that the church can recapture and teach to the community; after all, we know the true reason to celebrate. As we do this we get to express a part of our spirituality back to the community.

The final aspect that needs to be played out in the prayer life of the church is covenant. Theologically and ontologically the church is the people of God. Our origin, our reality and our destiny is tied to this fact. Covenant is simply an agreement between two parties. In the Christian faith we recognize two covenants, what we call the old, which was dominated by the law as a way into relationship with God, and the second made available to us through the death and resurrection of Jesus. This could be seen as a covenant of grace, although both really fall into that category. The covenant is like the framework in which we operate. I believe that God is present everywhere and can work through people who haven't professed faith however God extends a special relationship to us and for those who accept they enter into this covenant and in turn have a consciousness about God's goodness and his Kingdom's desire to create a better world for all.

If the church is to reflect a holistic spirituality it needs to embrace transcendence, intimacy, celebration and covenant as it relates to itself and its mission in the world. Scripture provides a good reference point for this journey.

Scripture

Any expression of church needs to be shaped by the witness of Scripture. Surprisingly to many this is not predominantly to do with doctrine or dogmatics, although these can be important reflections. The witness of Scripture that the church needs to embody is essentially a narrative that goes beyond science and reason and into the very depths of the purpose behind the universe. It's a narrative that explains not so much the nuts and bolts of creation, but the reason for it, and sets the incredibly relational God in his place as the God that creates, woos and longs to re-create all people. This narrative points out the need for renewal, due to people's desire to go their own way and tells the story of the process by which God was going to make all things right. The story is one of expectation and hope for the future, recognizing the good of the created order and God's presence with it. Then the gospels with their various takes on the person and work of Jesus, moving onto the birth of the church through the presence and work of the Spirit. The narrative also points to how God plans to wrap up this phase of eternity. The story clearly includes us and the role we have as we partner with God in the process of renewal.

I grew up in the evangelical Bible belt of Sydney and as such The Word was a big part of any church service. I always feel grateful for the grounding I received in The Word during those days and subsequent experiences at Bible college. However, I feel the broader narrative that we are only just touching on was not always simply in view. The danger of exegetical sermons, or even thematic teaching for that matter, is if they don't have an eye to the broader message of Scripture all kinds of subjective opinions can be pronounced as truth. I realize it is not as simple as that, with church culture, previous experiences, bias of the predominant culture all playing a part in any presumption of truth, but keeping the bigger story in context is a helpful corrective.

Much of this narrative can be framed through Kingdom language. Although problematic, there is very little else that describes the totality of God's reign and the renewing influence this reign seeks to have in the world. The Kingdom represents the in-breaking of God's future into the present. This reality needs to shape us as individuals, groups and whole gatherings. Like the encapsulation of holistic prayer, living as people of the Kingdom means that we embrace this totality and we let the revelatory and celebratory nature of this reality shape our gatherings and our impact on the world. As we hold this narrative, two things become evident. First, hope. Because of the presence of God with us now, we are hopeful that this world can be different. We are not only waiting for a new future but living in it now. And of course this present hope is a reflection of our ultimate hope, that one day God will complete the job of renewal. The second aspect of this narrative we need to hold is that God is for this world. He is invested in it and so therefore what happens in our time and space is of immense importance and all we do for the building of the Kingdom will travel with us into eternity. In the end heaven comes to earth, the renewal is brought about by the complete reign of God becoming manifest amongst us. What an incredible hope and reason for joy as we seek to make a Kingdom difference in the here and now.

Authenticity

According to McCrindle Research, the biggest reason why Australians don't go to church is that they see it as irrelevant to their life (47%). The second biggest reason is they don't accept how it is taught (26%).[10] There is room to debate what this second statistic is saying but I suspect it relates at least in part to views around authenticity and hypocrisy. Keith Miller, pastor and author, says,

> Our modern church is filled with many people who look pure, sound pure, and are inwardly sick of themselves, their weaknesses, their frustration and the lack of reality around them in the Church. Our non-Christian friends feel either 'that bunch of nice untroubled people would never understand my problems'; or the more perceptive pagans who know us socially or professionally feel that we Christians are either grossly protected and ignorant about the human situation or are out and out hypocrites who will not confess the sins and weaknesses (they know intuitively) to be universal.[11]

---

10. McCrindle Research, "Church Attendance in Australia," *McCrindle Blog*, 28 March, 2013, http://blog.mccrindle.com.au/the-mccrindle-blog/church_attendance_in_australia_ infographic.

11. Keith Miller cited in Michael Frost, *Exiles: Living Missionally in a Post-Christian Culture*, (Peabody, MA: Hendrickson, 2006), 97-98.

Sadly many in our churches have been conditioned to believe that they need to be inauthentic, that the fellowship of the believers is not a safe place to be truthful and vulnerable.[12] These feelings at least for me were mixed with the ego desire to be seen to have it all together. I particularly felt this pressure in Bible college as its staff sought to shape candidates for ministry in a particular way. Unfortunately I carried these feelings of it not being safe to be real and authentic into further ministry settings and to some degree am still battling to be fully real in environments where it would be helpful to do so.

Wright points out that there is a dichotomy here, seeing that we are called to be holy (set apart).[13] However in the pursuit of holiness, the gathered believers have often become spaces of unreality. Contrast this again with the biblical narrative, where we have very ordinary and flawed people being used by God to do extraordinary things. People like you and me experiencing real life with real struggles seeking to be honest before God. Perhaps as people of God we shouldn't be too hard on ourselves as we live in a world where appearance is everything and on first ask everyone is fine. Being inauthentic leads to alienation, particularly in the context of church and, with the example of the inclusive Trinity in the forefront of our minds, this isn't an acceptable space to create.

Alienation forms as an individual believer has the impression that Christians are shiny and perpetually happy. If that is not the case for this person then it becomes hard to act in that environment with any sense of integrity. Over time the environment becomes increasingly toxic for the believer as they see God blessing everyone else and not them. Walter Brueggeman suggests that this leaves a numbness and an ache, a yearning for something richer and more real and if not dealt with can lead to silent, unspoken rage, ultimately affecting someone's sense of wellbeing and self-worth.[14]

The antidote is to fashion communities of honesty, openness, hospitality and genuine love. Frost sees that to be effective these communities will hold to six values: spiritual growth that values inward transformation over external appearances; spirituality that doesn't limit creativity or individuality and values diversity and difference over conformity and

---

12. Frost, *Exiles,* 93.

13. Wright, *Surprised by Hope,* 296.

14. Walter Brueggeman cited in Frost, *Exiles,* 97.

uniformity; relationships marked by honest dialogues; a striving to be completely honest with God and appropriately transparent with others over our failings, transgressions and struggles as well as our hopes, dreams and emotions; an embracing of mystery and paradox and living with questions that don't have easy answers; a working to recalibrate our lifestyle holistically to reflect our hope for a more just, equitable and merciful society.[15]

As someone with evangelical heritage, my tendency is to want to provide answers for difficult questions, to explain away the paradoxes, but, as explored earlier, mystical or contemplative spirituality more easily lends itself to living with unanswered questions. We live in a postmodern world where people are skeptical of metanarratives that claim solutions to every issue, and so a more appealing way to connect with particularly Gen Ys and Millennials may be to stop trying to make our faith appear neat but emphasize its connection to the reality and mess of life. Within that framework it becomes much more straightforward to share our own reality and mess and acknowledge as Francis of Assisi did that we are all beggars in need of bread. This means that we can share our journey of transformation, not forgetting to mention that we are still in the process of becoming.

If we acknowledge that life and faith are messy we are less likely to think that everyone has to share the same understanding or practice as us and it leaves room for people to express their spirituality in a range of ways. In this paradigm honesty then becomes something our faith is known for. I was impressed a few years ago when a group of ministers from an outlying municipality in Melbourne decided to stand together and apologize to the women of the community for their lack of response to domestic violence. They acknowledged that they had swept issues under the carpet as desperate women approached them for solutions. Yes, it was tragic that these ministers did not respond appropriately at the time of encounter. However, their public repentance served the church in their community well.

This act also showed a commitment to a more just, equitable and merciful society.[16] Frost encourages us to examine our lives individually and corporately. On an individual level we need to explore our lifestyles, including diet and spending patterns, and ask how does our way of doing life compares with our desires for a better world, both in our interpersonal

---

15. Frost, *Exiles*, 100-101.
16. Frost, *Exiles*, 100-101.

relationships and more globally. These are challenging questions, but ones we need to face if we are to live authentic lives before our family, friends, neighbours, colleagues and others we come in contact with. Corporately we also need to explore how our gathered community provides for the need to be real with each other. This could include the formation of small accountability groups or giving permission and opportunity for people to just come as they are.

Small church tends to lend itself to doing this better, although it is not impossible in a larger gathering. Most of the small communities I've been a part of accept people just as they are, without the formality of needing to dress a certain way or participate along expected norms. There is great freedom in allowing someone just to come to the corporate gathering, in effect to meet God, just the way they are. In fact this becomes Christ's body, the church, modelling his open and accepting embrace, made so obvious by the cross.

Love

Above everything else, love is to be the central characteristic that the community of God is known for. When I get the opportunity to preach in a church service I quite often talk about a short passage in John's gospel (John 13:35) that seems to me at least to be a central shaping force for the life of the church. Jesus says to his disciples, 'they shall know you by the love you have for each other.' I challenge the congregations by saying this statement raises two questions for us. First, as a body do we love each other? This could be taken at an individual church level or - even more challenging - referring to the visible unity of the global church. The second question is, if we do love each other, how do people get to see that and be drawn towards the fellowship of the believers and ultimately Christ?

Some of the extra-biblical stories of the early church quite clearly show the commitment they had to each other. Acts talks about having everything in common, but there are also stories where the church was considered incestuous because of their close bonds and their habit of calling each other brother and sister. I'm not suggesting this would necessarily be helpful in our culture, but we have let the community aspect of church suffer in recent decades due to our capitulation to forces such as individualism, mobility (people frequently moving regions), the pursuit of wealth and somehow a lazy connectedness that in many cases is insipid at best and down right

104

superficial at worst. Perhaps we have also missed how the rhythms of the church year prepare us for loving community. However, this is the topic of a whole other book.

I suspect part of the reason for this lack of understanding around community is that many of us have not had strong loving community modelled to us and so we need to go back to first principles. We are dealing with two realities. The first is our present, and second, the future reality of the church. Living out love towards one another, as incomplete as it is, acts as a bridgehead between these two realities.[17] As well, of course, love towards each other acts as a pathway for others to follow towards the community of faith.

As we think about what it means to love each other, 1 Corinthians 13 is a good guide, explaining to us what love is, what it isn't, and some practical steps to being loving. Submerging ourselves and our congregations in passages like this allows us to breakthrough modern stereotypes of what it is to be loving. We use one word for this concept where the Hebrew world had four. So in one breath we can say we love ice cream and the next we love God or each other. Hopefully there is a difference in our hearts around this love. Although some ice cream is very good. Whilst I think it important for us to hear declarations of sacrificial love from each other, it will be the actions of love that draw us towards one another and others towards the well we are creating. Again, Scripture can be our guide as we reflect on the 'one another' passages, bearing each others' burdens and being prepared to love courageously even in the hard times, or love those amongst us who, let's face it, are very hard to love. And on any given day, that could be any one of us.

Reflecting ontologically on the love we are to have as a fellowship, because of Christ's work on the cross we already live in the bonds of love and we are moving towards this love being completed. So 1 Corinthians 13 is not another list of dos and don'ts, but a commentary of the reality we live in and a challenge to us to live it out as a reflection of what is to come. An important part of the living out is to practise forgiveness. In fact we won't be able to truly love the other if we don't have the capacity to give and receive forgiveness.

Seeing as we are being authentic I'll admit that I have had trouble forgiving those that have hurt me in the past. I have found it relatively easy to sweep

---

17. Wright, *Surprised by Hope*, 299-301.

the pain of their actions under the carpet and pretend in a sense there was no need to do the personal work to be able to let the resentment or whatever emotion go. This has inevitably backfired, with suppressed emotions erupting in other ways, sometimes quite unexpectedly. My inability to forgive has hampered my own ability to receive forgiveness, including Christ's, and has also affected my experience of joy and grief, shaded as they were by other emotions. In recent times it has been very freeing to begin untangling some of this web, that has held me captive. Of course in personal work such as this, forgiving oneself is as important as any other type of forgiveness.

As we individually do this work, we will be in a better place to live out some of Paul's other exhortations to love (Rom 12:5,10,16; 1 Thess 5:11; Gal 5:13; 6:2). Again, understanding that through the work of Christ God's future has broken into our present, the church is empowered to live this life of love through the unifying work of the Holy Spirit. This type of love does not cause us to be inward focused, concerned only for ourselves as a holy huddle, but is designed to be contagious and overflowing.[18] As John says, love is meant to be our strongest inner characteristic as well as our central message and demonstration to the world.

Love is also our core motivation for engagement with the world, whether it's our local community, city or a bigger global project. Love is also why we have to think about how we engage with the community. If we truly love someone and we see them in pain, we will not just want to apply a temporary bandaid or short term fix. We will want to promote their whole healing and work with them to ensure they don't re-descend into pain. Similar thinking lies behind good community development. It is not enough to feed someone, even house them or only meet other immediate needs (which we need to do for those in desperation) but together with them we need to set up ways for individuals and whole communities to heal and move away from the edge of marginalization. Many of the miracles that Jesus performed and the thrust of much of his teaching points in this direction.[19] Again the heart of this connection to the world is the love shared between members of the community of God. 'The community in its corporate life, is to embody an alternative social order that stands as a sign of God's redemptive purposes

---

18. Guder, ed., *Missional Church*, 149.

19. Ched Myers in *Binding the Strongman*, which is a political reading of Mark's gospel, alludes to these thoughts as one of Jesus' key motivations.

in the world: this is the concrete social manifestation of the righteousness of God.[20] Whilst this may start within the body of believers, because of the reality of the presence of God's Kingdom with us now, it can't stay there, but must permeate through all of society.

Hospitality

Henri Nouwen, in his ground breaking book on spirituality, *Reaching Out,* describes three movements that take place in the life of a disciple of Jesus: loneliness to solitude; hostility to hospitality; and illusion to prayer. He believes the order is important as we come home to ourselves, then others and ultimately God. Taking the second movement from hostility to hospitality, Nouwen understands that hospitality is not only to do with the spirituality of food, but the whole way we approach the other.[21]

Servants Community Housing based in Hawthorn, Melbourne, is an example of true hospitality. Over three large houses they accommodate around 90 people, most with mental health issues. Many of these people would otherwise be homeless. The environment they establish is based on love and respect for the stranger. Whilst there are house rules that need to be followed and shared meals, the resident is not expected to take part in any programs or look for work. They are not even preached to. Residents are treated with dignity and their autonomy respected. Around the residents there are live-in managers and others who connect regularly, essentially checking in to make sure people are doing ok. For the most part residents begin to feel safe, with some of their basic needs being met. After a time many begin to express desires to support community life or take steps toward transformation. The hospitality itself, the modelling of another way, the space to take it up or not is what in the end has been determinative in so many moving forward.

Hospitality is the heart attitude of compassion put into practice. Like love, it is what needs to underpin our engagement in the world. Whilst it may not feel proactive, if it is genuine and sustained, change in individuals will begin to occur, by their own volition, so much more powerful than any forced conformity. As a shaping force within churches, hospitality first needs to be

---

20. Richard Hays cited in Guder, ed., *Missional Church,* 149.

21. Henri J.M. Nouwen, *Reaching Out: Three Movements of the Spiritual Life,* (New York, NY: Doubleday, 1975), Chapter 4.

extended within the fellowship, welcoming those who are different without the expectation of conformity.

When I first moved to Adelaide I started attending a Baptist church. The community was very caring, particularly the older people would look out for and talk with the teenagers and young adults. However, there was a subtle pressure for those coming in to see life in the same way as the rather traditional approach that many of the regulars had. There didn't appear to be a lot of room to hold different opinions about life priorities, sexuality, dress and what was acceptable in church. One day someone in their twenties came to the church in crisis, his friend had just put himself through a plate glass window and this had rocked Geoff to the core.[22] His appearance was shabby and it was obvious things had been rough for him as there was a very plain-to-see upside down cross, etched into his forehead. After the initial crisis had been sorted and life was returning to a relative normal, Geoff stared regularly attending the church. He even began to bring a couple of friends. However over time, as hard as they tried to relate to Geoff and his friends, most of the congregation struggled to connect, as did Geoff. So whilst there was an initial welcome, the values of ordered engagement and the way church 'needed' to be done superseded the welcome. For a time a small group gathered outside of the rest of the life of the church (although supported by the pastor) to connect with and disciple each other. *Pizza, Poetry and Jesus* provided that sense of hospitality that saw a diverse range of people travel a discipleship journey together.

Going further Sider, Olson and Unruh emphasize a worthwhile goal echoed in Deuteronomy 15:4, stated simply, 'there will be no one in need among you.'[23] This is important for the same reasons that *Servants Community Housing* work to house people - the simple act of showing dignity and respect to another in the meeting of basic life requirements. Sadly in many congregations, often because of the need to appear as though everything is ok, basic needs of people in the church community go unmet. If these needs are not being met, inevitably people will feel insecure and not cared for. Feeling this way they are not likely to invest in the mission or witness of the community.

22. Name has been changed to respect privacy.

23. Ronald Sider, Philip Olson & Heidie Unruh, *Churches That Make a Difference: Reaching Your Community with Good News and Good Works,* (Grand Rapids, MI: Baker Books, 2002), 179.

As we know the first Christian Community recorded in Acts demonstrated this principle (Acts 2:44-45; 4:34). Interestingly, it was also love in action, drawing huge numbers towards the fellowship. If the church is to be an authentic witness to the benevolence of God's Kingdom, then the sharing of finances, goods, services and time needs to become a routine way of life. If we, the church in our country, could pull that off it would be an incredibly powerful counter-cultural witness.

Communitas – Shaping for Mission

Have you ever had an intense experience with a group of people? It might have been at work, where as a team you were heading towards a deadline and suddenly everyone kicks it up a gear, and it's like the realities of time and space and even your ordinary life disappear for a time and each person is focused on what they need to do to reach the goal. Or perhaps you were playing sport and it was coming right down to the line in a tied game and suddenly the team came together as a unit. This somewhat describes communitas, it goes beyond the experience of community to a deeper bond, usually created through some shared experience. War veterans describe this type of experience shared with their unit during combat or even training events. One of the causal factors of communitas is a phenomenon known as liminality.

The term was developed by anthropologist Victor Turner and has since been used by Christian writers such as Alan Roxburgh and Alan Hirsch to in part describe the experience of the church. It is a term that brings together both the church's inner shape and its outworking in mission to the world. Liminality applies to the situation where people (as individuals or a collective) find themselves in a transitional or marginal state in relation to the surrounding community or society. They are in that state as a result of their conscious awareness. Their status, role and place within society has been radically changed to the point that the group has now become largely invisible to that society. This space could involve significant danger or disorientation, but this is not essential for liminality. Victor Turner uses the example of the rite of passage for tribal boys on their way to manhood. This is a time where they are removed from the society of the tribe and are thrust into a situation where they have to fend for themselves, sometimes for a period of up to six months.[24] With a heightened sense of danger

---

24. Alan Roxburgh, *The Missionary Congregation, Leadership and Liminality,* (Harrisburg,

and urgency, the boys transitioning through the rite of passage emerge from being disorientated and individualistic to developing deep bonds of comradeship.[25]

Biblical history has shown that liminality and the resulting communitas has been the norm for God's people. Abraham was called to leave his known world and travel into a foreign land risking his household and reputation and forsaking much of the wealth produced by his lands. Journey becomes a common theme as the people of Israel leave Egypt for the promised land. Many of the prophets were wanders and tended to live in another reality compared to the rest of the people. Through to Jesus and the liminal experience he shared with his disciples through the highs and lows of his ministry. We also see liminality and communitas evidenced through Paul's ministry as he travels with his companions.

Throughout the history of the Church we have seen God's people banded together and flourishing through adversity. Communitas, then, 'happens in situations where individuals are driven to find each other through a common experience of ordeal, humbling, transition and marginalization. It involves intense feelings of social togetherness and belonging brought about by having to rely on each other in order to survive.'[26] In much of the modern era of the Church this sense of adversity has not been present, due largely to the Christendom experience, where we have been led to believe that we have been successful.

The reality is the Church has always been in a type of crisis, firstly ontologically and experientially as it has sort to grapple with the tension between its essential nature and current condition.[27] More recently, though, particularly in the west the Church has been in a cultural crisis as it has been perceived to be more and more irrelevant to modern life. This presents both a danger and an incredible opportunity. The danger is a gentle slide to non-existence. The opportunity is to re-invent ourselves as the people of God in this time and space; to once again experience liminality and communitas as we recognize the now and not yet of our existence, and work together with God towards stronger expressions of His kingdom in the here and now.

PA: Trinity Press, 1997), 23-24.

25. Liminality can occur in any group that experiences significant transition.

26. Roxburgh, *The Missionary Congregation, Leadership and Liminality*, 221.

27. Hendrik Kraemer cited in Bosch, *Transforming Mission*, 2.

In order for the church to effectively re-invent itself in our time and space we need to understand our culture and the journey it took to where it is now. In the next chapter we'll briefly explore the roots of postmodern culture, starting with the enchanted late medieval culture, through disenchantment, the effects of the Renaissance and into the development of our western culture. Then in the following chapter we will begin to draw the threads together and look at how we can respond in a way that recognizes both God's Kingdom agenda and the world in which we live. They may not be as far apart as you initially imagine!

Reflection Questions

1. I know there is at times a lot of talk about following other gods and it can feel a bit clichéd to talk about, however, what does it mean for you to live under the Christologically redefined shema, *love the Lord your God with all your heart, mind and strength*?

2. What part have buildings and your local area played in the expression of your church's mission? (Or that of your organization?)

3. As a church our internal attitude needs to be shaped by prayer, Scripture, authenticity, love, hospitality and communitas. How have the different churches you have been a part of gone at living those characteristics? (For those thinking about other organizations, how have they exhibited authenticity, love, hospitality and a cohesive, inclusive culture?)

4. None of us will ever reach the ideal church or organization, but from your exploration in question 3 what areas could your church or organization improve on? Concretely what would you do differently in order to engage more effectively with the community?

Chapter 6. - The Journey so Far: Understanding our Cultural Context

No one welcomes chaos, but why crave stability and predictability.
Hugh Mackay

The openness and complexity of life today can make finding meaning and the qualities that contribute to it - autonomy, competence, purpose, direction, balance, identity and belonging - extremely hard, especially for young people, for whom these are the destinations of the developmental journeys they are undertaking. ... Faced with a bewildering array of options and opportunities, we can become immobilized - or propelled into trying to have them all. Pulling together the threads of our postmodern lives isn't easy.
Richard Eckersley

The world we live in has been described as one of rapid discontinuous change, meaning not only are things changing at a pace that could potentially exhaust us all, but those changes are such that they threaten existing traditional authority or power structures. Essentially changing the way things are currently done or have been done for a long time.[1] This naturally breeds uncertainty and for some even disorientation as they try to negotiate banking and paying bills, using supermarkets, not to mention the whole advent and rise of online shopping. Even the way we access music continues to evolve at a rapid rate. These changes, whilst seeming minor to some, begin to change our psyche, subtly affecting the way we see the world and what is important to us. Of course change also happens on a broader scale as the bounds of the city catches up with once rural communities. Amy and I witnessed this first hand as Pakenham in the outer South East of Melbourne transitioned from a quiet inner country town, that a lot of Melbournians remember stopping at on their way to holidays in Gippsland, to a thriving and, at least to external appearances, prosperous community. Over a few years fields that once housed cows and horses transitioned to streets with housing lots. Many houses looking remarkably similar to

---

1. "Discontinuous Change," *Business Dictionary*, accessed 23 May, 2016, http://www. businessdictionary.com/definition/discontinuous-change.html.

each other and somehow all centred around water, both figuratively in their name, and literally. The biggest of these, Lakeside, had a man-made lake big enough to take small boats out on. Again, to many in Melbourne these changes were inconsequential yet to those who had lived in the community, some since birth, seeing their rural life disappear before their eyes was both disorientating and caused much grief. On the other side of the equation, change also occurred for those moving into the community, who I've referred to before, now living up to sixty kilometres away from work, recreation, family and so on. The scenario for the new arrivals was probably more hopeful, as they settled into a new way of doing life with all the ups and downs of establishing house and yard. Change of course is never easy and due to loss of a job or a relationship breakdown even in this prosperous outer suburb, poverty, heartache, isolation and disconnection was not too far away for some.

So how can the church connect with people going through rapid and disorientating change, as our culture both at times solidifies around particular events and at other times is liquid, sweeping us all up in its relentless forward momentum? In order to understand and discover how to connect meaningfully with our culture, the Church needs to comprehend and track the core significant changes and influences that have led to what we experience today. Charles Taylor outlines the transition of Western culture from a Christian era to a secular one, over a span of five hundred years. He relates this as a journey from the understanding and experience of people as being porous, that is open to the direct influence of the world around them and their beliefs about that world. He then traces their development to the modern concept of the self as 'buffered' against those forces and the experience of a plethora of belief options.[2]

Late Medieval Culture

In Medieval times the way the cosmos worked was set and unquestioned, with the hierarchical order being God, Church, King and Nobles, People, Animals, Plants and Objects. This was not tampered with and individuals and communities had to keep their proper place in relation to their God, the church and the ruling class.[3] In addition, the world was seen as 'enchanted',

---

2. Charles Taylor, *A Secular Age*, (Cambridge: Belknap of Harvard University, 2007). This is a summary of the intent of the book.

3. Bosch, *Transforming Mission*, 263.

with the existence of spirits, both good and bad. Natural events were viewed as acts of God and the mere existence of society was recognition of God's hand, so it was almost impossible to imagine a world without God.[4] The popular belief was that good and evil acted on the mind and either one could possess and take over it. Feelings were essentially determined by outside events, and in this way individuals were porous, they absorbed the world around them. God was seen as the ultimate good in an enchanted world. The option of living without God was simply not there.[5]

Some recent TV shows such as *Merlin*, *Vikings*, and others, although fiction, have provided some helpful windows into what life was like for medieval people. From their stand-point life appeared very hard and tedious for those living in towns or on the land who were just ordinary people. Yet this tediousness would not have been questioned. More, it would have been accepted by most as just the way it was. God had ordained it to be this way.

With God seen as the foundation of society, a key building block became conformity. Because of the porous nature of the medieval mind, the individual could not break away from the responsibilities and benefits of being a part of society. If they were to stand outside these things, they believed inevitably something bad would happen. This was at least in part manifested through their understanding of good and bad magic. In this equation God was seen as the ultimate good and, therefore, standing outside of the order that God had established would lead to unhelpful consequences. There was also a sense that the common good was bound up in collective rites, devotions and allegiances. The collective nature was such that if one person stood outside of these beliefs and did not practice them, then all of society could reap the negative consequences, and in fact the whole structure of society would be brought into question. God was seen to have an existentially foundational role in society and as such it was impossible to conceive the thought that society could exist if it were not grounded in common religious beliefs.[6]

These beliefs led to a tension between two goals within medieval society - transcendence and human flourishing. In the medieval understanding, the Christian faith pointed towards a self-transcendence, a life beyond human

---

4. Taylor, *A Secular Age*, 25.

5. Taylor, *A Secular Age*, 32-41.

6. Taylor, *A Secular Age*, 43.

flourishing, and yet the institutions of society were at least partly attuned to foster human flourishing. Looking at medieval society critically, it is easy to see the struggle between the two tensions. Erasmus pointed out that even in seeking piety many were looking to their own benefit. People were even following special religious rites in a superstitious way, hoping to fend off evil spirits or receive some kind of blessing.[7] To Erasmus this was idolatry.

The tension between transcendence and human flourishing is also linked to the hierarchical complementarity of the structure of society at that time. Not all experienced the same dignity with various positions or functions expected to serve others. The celibate professions were seen to be near the top of the hierarchy. 'The clergy pray for all, the lords defend all, the peasants labour for all' is a formula that highlights these complementary functions.[8] Taylor argues therefore in medieval society there was a place for something less than the highest vocation and aspirations, which led to the creation of an equilibrium. Of course this was founded on the flourishing of some and the subservience of others.

From time to time this tight structured medieval equilibrium needed to let chaos reign. Otherwise, like a pressure cooker without a valve, it would explode. Chaos was seen as the enemy as well as the energy behind the organization of the community. That is community was organized so tightly, so chaos could not reign. Victor Turner, borrowing from Thomas Merton, observes that every so often the patterned arrangements of role sets, status sets and status sequences needed to be suspended.[9] If this was not the case, the fight against chaos would so weaken ordered society to the point that it became ineffectual. In medieval culture the safety valve was the carnival or festival. These times of celebration created communitas, the underlying sense that despite the formality of very structured and coded relationships, people were essentially human and equal.

Another great leveler in medieval society was time and how it related to eternity. There were two concepts of eternity. One based on Plato's understanding, in which God gathers everyone in an instant, and so there was a rising out of the time that we experience. Medieval thought saw this to be a lifting to the time of the gods. There was also the understanding that

---

7. Erasmus cited in Taylor, *A Secular Age*, 45.

8. Taylor, *A Secular Age*, 45.

9. Thomas Merton, used by Victor Turner cited in Taylor, *A Secular Age*, 47.

time ran horizontally and vertically. Horizontal time is what we experience as normal. Through vertical time one could have experiences that were closer to God's eternal paradigm or be further away. Closer experiences would include times in church and religious events. Those times further away from God's eternal paradigm were characterized by chaos.[10] All of medieval society was affected by these different experiences of time. However their world began to change.

The Enchanted Mind

The Medieval psyche was shaped mainly by the hierarchy of social order that I mentioned earlier. These assumptions led to the conclusion that God was foundational to life. God was seen as the ultimate good and the protector amongst a society fraught with fear and bad magic. If someone sought to shake this equilibrium, they were not only affecting themselves but bringing all of society's order into question, thus they would be quickly cast out. In all of this the psyche of the individual was porous, they were acted upon by the forces of the world. They did not see themselves as autonomous but more as victims (although I don't think they would have used that word, as they had no consciousness of anything other) of the good and evil around them.

To alleviate the pressure of an ordered society there was the carnival or festival, where chaos was allowed to reign, which ultimately kept the tumult in check. They saw the world as enchanted and understood time in a way that pointed to God's activity in that world. Contrasting this with today's psyche where the sense of the collective has broken down and individuals see themselves as buffered from the forces around them, and the belief has shifted from seeing themselves as acted upon to being able to choose responses to those forces. Of course in our modern world even those forces have been reinterpreted. What once might have been considered an evil spirit might today be seen as a mental illness.

Road to Disenchantment

During late medieval Europe there were many reform movements. Taylor describes it as a 'rage for order'.[11] There was a desire to see society lifted up to a higher way of being and functioning. Latin Christendom was no

---

10. Taylor, *A Secular Age*, 58-59.

11. Taylor, *A Secular Age*, 63.

exception and through its own reforms led the way to the partly secularized ideal of civilization that we live amongst today.[12] As civilization dawned through the late medieval and early modern period, reforms within Christendom were crucial to the disenchantment of the world and the rise of exclusive humanism. One key factor was the development of doctrine and the internalizing of faith. Previous to this faith was seen as simple understandings and actions. Doctrines increased Christianity's complexity and the external and communal aspects, whilst remaining present gave way to the inner experience of faith. Not a bad development in and of itself, but from here we can trace the beginnings of a shift from a religious age to a secular one. This shift included more complex reasoning around the nature of God and his action in the world. As well, prayer became an inner reality from which meditative practices evolved. From around 1000 CE people's understanding of faith began to again centre around Christ and 1215 CE as a result of the Lateran Council, priests were encouraged and equipped to better train the laity. There were also itinerant friars who were often better educated than parish priests, and they were able to propagate new teachings and practices.

A doctrine formative to Christianization of the western world, individuation and the forming of a new understanding of civilization was the teaching on death. Medieval culture saw death as a continuation of life, a lesser stage, but still holding a continuity to the previous stage. They believed that the deceased were close by and were jealous of the living and could come back and haunt them. Because of this closeness, whilst not welcomed, there was no real reason to fear death. It was seen as just the next stage. The Christian understanding showed that there was something beyond human flourishing in this life, after death, and that there was a judgment before one could enter into this beyond. Once the teaching became popular a fear of death became mediated into the medieval world with a sense that one may not measure up or be allowed to experience the riches of heaven. It also pointed to the individual's responsibility for their response to the Christian call, judgment and transformation.[13]

At the same time that this belief was permeating civilization, life was changing. Peasants were leaving villages to live in towns and take up work

---

12. Taylor, *A Secular Age*, 63.
13. Taylor, *A Secular Age*, 67.

in newly forming industries such as manufacturing, commerce, law and administration. As traditional cadres or groups broke down, the insular village mentality of people was beginning to broaden. Taylor argues that this led to an individuation, and a reinterpreting of understandings on issues such as death. The disenchantment process is very complicated, and holds many dichotomies, however, as people began to work out their own destiny and strive for their own riches, an increasingly wide gulf formed between human flourishing and the teachings of the Church. Human flourishing moved more to securing personal wealth and position, with the Church beginning to lose influence over the lives of individuals.

Meanwhile the Church itself was also changing. In an effort to create a purer form of faith, it was bringing into question many of its beliefs and practices. The new clergy saw themselves as boundary police, holding the tension between the illicit and legitimate uses of ritual (i.e. bringing to an end things like the selling of indulgences). They argued it wasn't enough to light a candle to a saint, but that to worship them one needed to follow in their footsteps in word, deed and practice.[14] Over time church magic became illegitimate, God was seen to have the naked power over all magic. This naked power was evident in the Judaism of the Old Testament and so in the late medieval period people's fear transferred from bad magic to fear of God. Through this process the fear of bad magic and the fear of the hierarchy of the Church were reversed at the same time. This began to change the nature of mass piety, that is why people were coming to church and what that meant in the broader society. The sacraments became truly symbolic, authority moved from the hierarchy back to Scripture and the visible church became distinguished from the true community of the saved. Through these dual sociological and ecclesiological processes society to a large degree lost its enchantment and the Church was ripe for reform.

The Effect of Science and Rationalism on Western Culture

It is not the purpose of this book to map changes in the Church over the centuries, except for when those changes impacted on society. The Reformation certainly impacted on society and in such a way that it began to destroy the unity and power of the Western Church and started a process which saw it lose its validating right over the structure of society. I'm sure Martin Luther was aware of the significance of nailing his theses to the door

---

14. Taylor, *A Secular Age*, 72.

of that German church, but he couldn't have known the unravelling effect that his act would have. Many would argue, and I would agree, that this unravelling needed to happen and that it was the beginning of the demise of Christendom, although its death pangs would last for many centuries. However as the Church became disunified it lost its position of validating right and wrong over society. This validation right moved directly to the king and through the king to the people.[15] As a result of the Reformation an equally significant change took place, with people being able to relate directly to God. In society this began to translate as the early stirrings of democracy. In addition, with the dawn of the scientific age people discovered that they could ignore God and nothing bad happened. Through this a significant shift occurred, people began to look for the meaning of their existence in the natural order: from below, not from above.

The period known as the Enlightenment was beginning to dawn. Two ways of thinking characterized this period - the Empiricism of Bacon and the Rationalism of Descartes. Neither thinker saw their thought as jeopardizing the Christian worldview, but in the period following their work, science took on more of an opposing stance when it came to faith. A dichotomy was created between faith and reason. Bosch points out that human reason was seen as part of the natural order and became less tied to the tradition and presuppositions of the past.[16] The porous psyche of the middle ages, where people believed forces acted upon them, was beginning to shift to the buffered self of the modern era where one is freer to respond to the forces of the world. Although you could argue that other forces have trapped our psyche... anyway, that is an unhelpful tangent for now.

Enlightenment thinking also operated within a subject-object framework. Previously people understood that they were linked to others and their environment through the medieval hierarchy explored earlier. The Enlightenment allowed people to view themselves as separate from their environment, which enabled them to explore it more objectively. Thus the continued forming of the buffered self, highlighted by Taylor.[17] Importantly creation became the subject of analysis, broken down into parts and ceasing to be a teacher. Even humanity was broken down into different components,

---

15. Bosch. *Transforming Mission*, 263.
16. Bosch, *Transforming Mission*, 264.
17. Taylor, *A Secular Age*, 131.

120

with the emergence of various disciplines such as philosophy, sociology, anthropology and various forms of physical sciences. There seemed no limit to what the human mind could comprehend. A new age was dawning. With the discovery of new continents it felt like the earth could be subdued. Humanity took on a new confidence, with the perception that what was real was only now beginning to manifest.[18]

A third characteristic of the Enlightenment was that purpose was taken from science. This started a trend that saw teleology (study of purpose of phenomena rather than cause) removed from much of public life. In the scientific world, focus shifted to causality. Ancient Greek and medieval science saw teleology as a vital category in their understanding of what they termed, animated causality. However, with the onset of modern thought, science ceased to ask questions relating to purpose, instead favouring cause and effect. In general, science believes in set and mathematically stable laws that guarantee a desired outcome. In this way science became mechanistic and associated with reason. Interestingly, today we are beginning to see a trend back to a connection between science and purpose with a moral call for the Church and other groups to be part of vetting science and putting some perspective on debates between the 'can' and 'should' of advancement.

As time has progressed there has been a lessening of the influence of faith in the public square as reason has risen. Newbigin argues though that the association of science as the only source of reason has been a misnomer and that the greatest advances in science have in fact come through intuition and imagination, or believing in the possibilities. Scientists will argue, based on modern thought, that scientific discovery comes through observing the facts, arriving at a hypothesis, and from this deducing consequences which can be further observed.[19] However, Newbigin rightly asserts that discovery in this way is really a matter of faith, or believing in what yet can't be seen. Newbigin helps us to see that the divide between faith and reason may not be as wide as first perceived.

Because of the scientific belief that reason is only determined through a set of facts, a divide did open up between science and religion. Over time science and scientific thinking became pervasive in society. With the rise of modernism, the cycle of life so central to medieval thought became

18. Taylor, *A Secular Age,* 264.
19. Bertrand Russel, cited in Newbigin, *Gospel in a Pluralist Society,* 30.

lessened to a biological and sociological process.[20] Science was also seen as factual, value free and neutral, although one could debate whether this was ever the case. The same couldn't be said for religion. Facts were seen as objectively true, outside of the mind of the believer. Facts determined whether a belief was true or not. Values on the other hand were seen to be opinion and a preference of choice, and so religion moved from the place of undisputed fact to the realm of belief and value, as it could not be proven. It was moved to the private world of the individual and no longer held its place of privilege in the public sphere. This space was left to science and the world of fact.[21]

Taylor further examines this inward move of faith, recognizing that whilst science was moving people to 'rational fact' religion itself was also going through the process of privatization. Within the Church there was a move towards more inward and intense personal devotion, a growing uneasiness with the 'magic' element of the sacraments and an embracing of Martin Luther's notion of 'salvation by faith.' Coupled with the advances in science this led to a reversal of the concept of an enchanted cosmos and opened the door to a humanist alternative.[22]

Humanism became manifest in the confidence of modern society, leading to many discoveries and the era of colonization. People believed they had the ability and the will to remake the world in their own image. Anything was possible! This saw the western model of technological development, based on the ideal of modernization imposed on developing countries. In effect this meant the focus was on material possession, consumerism and economic advance. The belief was that these things would trickle down to the poorest of the poor and each would get their fair share of the wealth being generated. Through this the message given to the developing countries was that they were backward, undeveloped peoples and this should be overcome and left behind.[23] Whilst the intentions of modern economics might have been good, the outworking was not positive, with selfishness and a lust for power becoming the predominant motif of the Western colonizers.

---

20. Bosch, *Transforming Mission*, 265.
21. Bosch, *Transforming Mission*, 266.
22. Taylor, *A Secular Age*, 76-77.
23. Bosch, *Transforming Mission*, 265-266.

Despite this, the new confidence in humanity led to a positivism which held, in principle, that all problems were solvable. The yet unsolved problems simply meant that all the relevant facts had not been mastered and it was only a matter of time until the freed and inquisitive human mind brought those too under control. In this way science was seen as the sum of all human existence. Its influence continued to increase in proportion with the available observational data. Through scientific understanding the rate of new inventions and discoveries rapidly increased in comparison to previous epochs. These advances finally meant that the external forces of nature were succumbing to human planning and reason. It of course also led to the exploitation of the natural world, the effects of which we are now struggling to reverse.

At the time of these advancements humans were able to remake the world in their own image and had clearly moved from being porous (acted upon), to being buffered, in control of their environment and acting volitionally. The individual was seen as emancipated and autonomous, in contrast to the middle ages where the community took priority over the individual.[24] Central to the Enlightenment, human progress was assured because of the competition of individuals pursuing their own happiness. Each human being was seen as perfectible and needed to be allowed to grow in line with his or her own choice. The desire for individualism and freedom had almost become an expected right in every Western democracy, and was valued over social responsibility. These beliefs and their outworking were a forerunner to postmodern relativism.

In this environment the believer faced many difficulties as they tried to live a life based on absolutes, in a space liberated from the tutelage of God and church. Also in this environment there was no privilege or legitimization for certain titles. All were considered equal, deriving their rights from nature and not religion. There was a dichotomy of understanding, people believed that they were more important than God, yet not fundamentally different to animals and plants. Thus they became open to being degraded to the status of machines that could be manipulated and exploited by others.[25]

Through the disenchantment process and the rise of science and rationalism, Western society gradually moved from Christendom to a secular ideal of

24. Bosch, *Transforming Mission*, 267.
25. Bosch, *Transforming Mission*, 267.

civilization. This process led to an internalizing of faith and the development of a new fear of death. Urbanization led to an individuation of people, and a breakdown of community structures which saw simultaneously the fear of hierarchy and the fear of bad magic diminish. This fear was placed onto God who had the power to deny transcendence beyond death. However over time, the validation of life, previously attributed to God, moved to the King and then to the people. Humanity realized they could ignore God and nothing bad would happen. The rise of science meant people and the world became objects to be studied, things were broken down into their components and science removed the question of meaning from its frame of reference. In society generally, confidence increased and there was a positivism that saw all problems as solvable. Humans were emancipated and free to travel their own path. And so the journey continued towards postmodernism.

The Journey Continues – Postmodern Culture

All of this is a backdrop to the current culture that we find ourselves in, one defined by postmodernity. Just as Enlightenment and modernist thinking led to a disenchantment, writers such as Zygmunt Bauman argue that postmodernity is a re-enchantment of the world, with its focus on representation.[26] By representation I mean a recognition that words and language hold certain meanings for us, and so mediate reality. But these meanings can be deconstructed and presented to us in different ways, thus shifting our sense of reality and asking questions about the nature of truth. In technical language this is about signification, which is particularly prevalent in our media soaked world. We are also living in a time that values the symbolic meaning of a product, job or some other status symbol as much if not more than the actual thing itself.

Postmodernity began in the avant-garde artistic and literary circles of the late 1950s and early 1960s. Artists began to play with non-representational or more abstract art. Much of this art was such that it could be deconstructed. The concept being represented could be broken down to its subsequent parts and re-interpreted differently by the observer, again bringing into question ultimate truth. This practice moved art theory and practice

---

26.   Zygmunt Bauman cited in Colin Greene and Martin Robinson, *Metavista: Bible, Church and Mission in an age of Imagination,* (Milton Keynes: Authentic Media, 2008), 25.

towards a post-structuralism, moving away from conventional semiology or interpretations of concepts through particular language.

As well there was an increase in reflexive expression where art was created in part to make a critical comment on the medium. The impact of this genre of course continues today with satirical cartoons like *The Simpsons* commenting on the power of TV in general. Linked to this is the concept of simulacrum. This refers to a representation of reality that is not quite real anymore. Reality TV is a classic example of this concept. Take for argument's sake *The Farmer Takes A Wife* or *The Bachelor*. Both portray the idea of meeting some exotic stranger, falling in love during romantic interludes and eventually discovering a life partner. These things are mediated to us as reality, yet somehow we all know intuitively that in the 'real' world meeting a life partner is not quite like that.[27]

Postmodern art started as a reaction to modern thought and art with its set model of semiology (structuralism), as well as disillusionment with a modernity that promised to create a better world. As mentioned earlier, with the Enlightenment and the rise of science, an optimistic humanism pervaded human thought. There was a belief that any problem was solvable, if in the present that didn't seem to be the case, then it was only a matter of time til all the pieces of the puzzle were discovered and fitted together in the correct sequence. However, after two world wars, a major economic depression and the beginning of the cold war, there was significant disillusionment about the human enterprise.

The Enlightenment understanding of reason and rationality was beginning to crumble and was not seen as an adequate cornerstone upon which to build life. The objectivist framework that had guided rationality resulted in a massive reductionism that quenched the human spirit. In the expanding of rationality, language and the use of metaphor, myth and analogy had been rediscovered. Along with this was the realization that science and theology were to probe, not prove the way the universe works.[28] There was the dawning of the understanding that rationality could be found in

---

27. The technical terms and concepts in the above two paragraphs were summarized in a lecture delivered by Dr. Penelope Trotter, Australian Catholic University, St Patrick's Campus, Melbourne, 2014.

28. Bosch, *Transforming Mission*, 353.

narrative and that in fact it was a better way to invoke the human spirit to action.

Narrative storytelling is a key component in postmodern culture, but the narrative is always sourced from a number of different components. Because of this and its roots in the aesthetic (arts) much of postmodern philosophy is espoused through movies and other forms of art. An archetypical movie and classic example is *The Matrix,* whose philosophical underpinnings include Plato, Descartes, Friedrich Nietzsche, Jean Lyotard and Jean Baudrillard.[29]

Postmodern thought draws on the work of key philosophers such as Friedrich Nietzsche, Michel Foucault and Jean Lyotard, who argue that there is no fundamental belief that underpins all of humanity or any particular facet of it. In their thinking science does not have a metanarrative and so is simply a series of pragmatic disciplines devoid of epistemological foundations and so becomes based on performance.[30] That is, how something acts. Science is not particularly interested in the why, unless that too is mechanistic. Previously, the metanarratives held by science were, first, the doctrine of human progress that saw the natural and human science advancing humanity towards emancipation form the limitations of the past. The second narrative is philosophically based and refers to the search for knowledge being a feature of the divine spirit's odyssey to lose itself in the other. Where the other refers to the whole history of humanity and our pursuit of knowledge in and of itself.[31]

With the de-bunking of these narratives, the range is clear for philosophers like Lyotard and Rorty to target any notion that there are transcendent universal principles or moral imperatives that undergird not only the pursuit of knowledge but society generally. Linking closely then with this thinking is the rise of consumerism. The consumer culture favours the aestheticization of life, assuming that the aesthetic life is the ethically good life and that this is the ideal to be sought after, instead of some greater purpose.[32] Almost without society noticing, commodities ceased being items of utility, transcended being items of luxury and became associated

---

29. Greene and Robinson, *Metavista,* 26.

30. Greene and Robinson, *Metavista,* 36.

31. Greene and Robinson, *Metavista,* 36.

32. Mike Featherstone cited in Greene and Robinson, *Metavista,* 28.

with fashionable brand identities. They have become fetishes associated with lifestyle, individual and group identities and technological innovations. They even support subversive elements that resist the status quo. Western society has been so enveloped by the ideology of consumerism that it has become our frame of reference.

Jean Baudrillard believes that consumerism has moved through a number of crucial stages and is now a sophisticated and coded system of meaning, dominated by what the product represents.[33] In this way consumerism plays with aspirations and clouds the boundaries between reality and fantasy. Baudrillard argues that the media has become the new power broker in the world of the hyperreal (distorted or exaggerated reality) and with its influence, the boundary between commodity and its sign value has imploded entirely. Sigmund Freud's understanding of the energies of the libido makes sense in this context as the consumer is *aroused* through visceral and iconic means that penetrate to a subliminal level and affect desire and motivation.[34]

In light of the postmodern landscape, the core question for philosophers is, how do we know what we know is true? The foundations upon which true knowledge was based have been discarded or re-interpreted and largely sensation and experience have taken the place of the search for truth and right. A brief exploration of the thought of Richard Rorty, Jean Lyotard and Jean Baudrillard will give a picture of the postmodern understanding of knowledge and truth.[35]

Richard Rorty reflects a laid back American pragmatism, claiming that the epistemology of modernity led to the unsubstantiated notion that the mind could actually mirror reality. He saw the enlightenment thinkers using knowledge to manipulate the world for their own purposes. Agreeing with Friedrich Neitzsche, he believed this was a particular society or culture's will to power. Rather, what is needed is the pragmatic ability to accept that each society or community utilizes epistemological procedures and language games to remain true to its own institutions and cultural practices. There are no epistemological or moral certainties to uncover.[36]

---

33. Jean Baudrillard cited in Greene and Robertson, *Metavista,* 29.

34. Greene and Robinson, *Metavista,* 31.

35. Greene and Robinson, *Metavista,* 33.

36. Richard Rorty cited in Greene and Robertson, *Metavista,* 33-35.

Jean Lyotard holds an incredulity towards metanarratives. Like Rorty, he objected to thinkers and scientists who claimed an objective scientific rationality that supposedly led to an account of how things really are. In his work he exposed science to be based upon metanarratives of legitimization. As mentioned above, these include the doctrine of human progress. The more we know about the world the freer humanity will be. Secondly, the philosophical story that sees the search for knowledge as a feature of the divine Spirit's attempt to find itself in the other. The other in this case is the whole history of humanity and the pursuit of knowledge in and for its own sake. In this way science is the realization of the divine reason and therefore based on the principle of universal knowledge. However, debunking this, he saw that consensus was not only impossible, but not desirable; that knowledge and truth was in dis-sensus which allowed for an ever increasing awareness of the contingent and localized.[37] If we think missiologically for a moment this highlights the importance of understanding the context in which we work or are about to enter.

Jean Baudrillard, as alluded to earlier, focuses on the destructive power of hyperreality. He sees that the media has destroyed both public and private space, bombarding both spaces with information that inhibits communication. He sees that through advertising, marketing, television and the internet the real is simulated, thus creating the hyperreal, which in turn collapses all distinctions between the real and the simulated. In the contemporary world, society is enticed to live in the hyperreal, responding to various stimuli that have the appearance of reality.[38]

Through this very brief foray into the inner workings of the postmodern mindset I have sought to demonstrate the complexity of the world we live in and the need to re-do our understanding of the cultural maps we follow as we think about engaging with our community. We need to do this as organizations, whether we come from a Christian or church base or one centred more in the social sciences.

The State of Western Society and the Role of the Church

Whilst institutions such as academia, politics, economics and the sciences recognize that society has moved from a modernist world view with its

---

37. Jean Lyotard cited in Greene and Robertson, *Metavista*, 35-36.
38. Jean Baudrillard cited in Greene and Robinson, *Metavista*, 37-38.

humanistic positivism to a post modern mindset that questions anything that claims to have truth or ultimate knowledge, the average member of society is positioned somewhere in the middle. Contemporary western society is largely characterized by a blending of modern and postmodern thought and action. Through my work in local communities I have witnessed firsthand the destructive effect of hyperreality. Distorted as it is by the high prevalence of all forms of media it has then been processed through the subject-object framework of modern rationalistic thinking. This has led to a black and whiteness that has completely justified a lifestyle that puts the pursuit of perceived affluence and the aesthetic over family and community. The generational poor in the South Eastern suburbs of Melbourne have also been affected by this blending of major epistemologies. From a place where the poor are essentially devoid of hope, social services often expect them to achieve goals that appear rational, yet are based on empiricism, ascribe to modernist goals of self-determination, yet expect people to respond from a narrow framework of what is true for them, totally unconnected to any enduring story.

Newbigin, writing in the late 1980s, speaks into this confusion, highlighting what Peter Berger identifies as plausibility structures. They are patterns of belief and practice that have been accepted within a given society. These structures determine what beliefs and actions make sense within a given community at a given time.[39] Coming from a Christian tradition, some of the plausibility structures of the Church are radically different to those in the general community. The task in front of the Church is to truly understand those structures of epistemology within a community or a society and use rational thought, as Newbigin sees it, to translate an understanding of the faith in such a way as it makes sense within those structures.[40] Newbigin argues for an holistic approach that encompasses social action and conversion as necessary parts of the Church's response.

For an organization that doesn't hold to the Christian worldview, understanding plausibility structures is still very important. For example, many larger social service organizations have a tendency to transplant services from one community to the next, regardless of whether the

---

39. Peter Berger cited in Newbigin, *Gospel in a Pluralist Society,* 8.

40. Newbigin argues that rational thought does not solely belong to the scientific world and that thought within a tradition such as Christianity is also rational. He argues this on the basis of plausibility structures.

community wants or needs that particular service. Funding is sought often in regions identified by state or federal government, organizations apply and then they deliver the service, with very little research or understanding of that particular community and how it works, and what would be truly effective.

The Church also has to examine its plausibility structures, looking to expand its paradigms of what is valid action in the community. Again, through my work in communities, I have witnessed the Church being passionate about individual conversion, yet silent on systemic poverty, social imbalance and political injustice. This has left many mystified about the role of the Church and its place in society. If our desire is to see people take hold of the Church's plausibility structures, and accept faith as a valid proposition, there needs to be a broadening of approach that recognizes a fuller Kingdom mandate as outlined in previous chapters.

If the Church was to accept the Kingdom goals of justice, beauty and evangelism, and worked in harmony with Kingdom values such as generosity, hospitality, intrinsic worth, forgiveness and freedom, it would begin to naturally embrace community development as a strategy for the expansion of God's Kingdom. Or to put it another way, the creation of a just society. From the community's point of view it would be seen in reverse. They would see a proactive church, working within a mutually understood plausibility structure, inviting others to partner in developing a just society using community development principles and practices. In turn these actions would point to God's Kingdom and faith would be validated as a viable option within the community's own plausibility structure.

So often our churches and social services in general fail to take into account the community's view of them. However, I suspect if they broadly adopted plausibility structures that made sense in the life of the community wherever it was and through this became more visible in that community some resistance and trust issues would be broken down.

With the need to understand local communities, the following chapters seek to provide a broad framework for engagement and begin to shift our focus to the practicalities of a strength based approach to community development.

Reflection Questions

1. Where have you experienced rapid discontinuous change? How did it leave you feeling?

2. Our contexts seem to be a mix of modernity and postmodernity, which can leave anyone feeling confused. What are some examples of how this has played out in your mission?

3. Whilst postmodernity is skeptical of the metanarrative it does seem to have created an openness to spirituality. How does this both help and hinder your mission? What changes do we need to make in our approach in order to be seen as relevant in this context?

4. Newbigin talks about plausibility structures. Spend some time thinking through your own, those of your church or organization and those of the community in which you work. What differences or similarities are there? What needs to be done in order to create meaningful partnerships?

Chapter 7. – Time to Get Practical

Every single person has capabilities, abilities and gifts. Living a good life depends on whether those capabilities can be used, abilities expressed and gifts given. If they are, the person will be valued, feel powerful and well-connected to the people around them. And the community around the person will be more powerful because of the contribution the person is making.
                    John P. Kretzman and John L. McKnight

So could I bring you full circle to once again consider your own context and that of the broader Australian society? In the opening chapter of this book I highlighted the social environment for young people, encouraging us to see it as a litmus test for how we are going as a nation. We also explored Appreciative Inquiry (AI), which starts with the strengths of the community and seeks to address issues through a lens that believes in the possibility of individuals and the strength of communities. I also pointed out that even proponents of AI don't ignore the issues but simply choose to start with the positives, recognizing that within our communities there are two realities represented by the positives and negatives that we acknowledge.

Sitting in those realities is God's dream or desire for our communities and indeed for the whole world. Passages such as Isaiah 58, 65 and Luke 4 clearly show a world of peace, security, prosperity, one where people are seen and valued, where there is justice and where compassion and mercy are normal. As part of his high school studies in politics my son had to put together a one page political ideology. He called his 'Compassionism.' On reading it to us he said it was hopelessly idealistic, yet it reminded me of these passages and seemed to be in line with God's non-politicized dream for the world. Perhaps God is the ultimate idealist. However, the reality of his dream was embodied by Jesus, showing us it wasn't just pie in the sky, so to speak. Jesus not only modelled the realized potential of God's longings but pointed us towards being part of this realization in his teachings on the Kingdom and his command to seek its manifestation above everything else (Matt 6:33).

God invites his people into active participation towards the reality of His Kingdom come. Through being part of the new creation, we are the first fruits, participants in and signposts to God's ultimate future. As such, we are given the task of building for the Kingdom. How are we to understand this task? What does this mean for the Church's engagement with the world? In the previous chapter I described Berger's concept of plausibility structures. These apply both in the Church and in broader society. Using this language, to help society see Christian faith as a plausible alternative, the Church needs to embrace a broad approach to community transformation. This is compatible with Asset Based Community Development (ABCD), the principles of which are expressed well in Liberation Theology.

Liberation Theology

> They [the church] wanted us to give food out to malnourished mothers and children, but they didn't want us to question why we were malnourished to begin with. They wanted us to grow vegetables on the tiny plots around our houses, but they didn't want us to question why we didn't have enough land to feed ourselves.
>
> Elvia Alvarado

I have had a long time interest in liberation theology, ever since living in the northern suburbs of Adelaide, a community consisting of many long-term unemployed families, including those that over three to four generations had never held a job. Families ripped apart by poverty, drug abuse and domestic violence. Families that people looked at and blamed for their situation, rather than seeing them as collective victims of a system that had largely ignored them and relegated them to a certain standing in life. Moving from the middle class beachside suburbs to this environment, rather than being confronting (although parts were), I felt it was actually refreshing. There was an honesty about this community not present in where I'd come from. What you saw was what you got. People were not afraid to tell you how it was, and anyway it was obvious.

With that backdrop I began to wonder what it would be like to write theology through this lens. I think I may have even produced a paper, now lost in the ether. However in the context of this current journey that we are taking together, liberation theology provides a good bridge for us to walk over towards effective community engagement and the application of ABCD.

Originating as part of the Catholic Church's response to the struggles of the poor and oppressed in Latin America, liberation theology provides a helpful connection between the Church and Kingdom orientated community transformation. Starting in praxis, it understands the need to live faith authentically and contextually. Leonardo Boff and Clodovis Boff provide a helpful overview of the process and principles of liberation theology. The process that the follower of Jesus embarks on as they take liberation theology seriously, is a similar process as for the church wishing to use ABCD.

Theology in Praxis

The starting place for liberation theology is a commitment to the poor. This commitment needs to be lived out with the people in their struggle for freedom from oppression. The theological practitioner actually participates in the process of liberation. Liberation theologians see this as a living link between theory or faith and practice or love.

The theologian then goes through three mediations in the development of a relevant theology grounded in orthopraxis. The first mediation is *social*. This is akin to community research and explores the social and historical context of the oppressed, essentially asking, why are they oppressed? This is a crucial question, the answer to which will shape our attitude to the poor and how we receive them into the faith community. There are three broad answers, which lead to different responses. These responses can be seen in various arms of the Church, particularly those that offer welfare, without an understanding of context. If one believes that the cause of poverty is empirical, that is, it's seen as vice, laziness, ignorance or sin, the poor are to be pitied and aid is the answer. If the cause of poverty is seen as functional, the poor are considered backward and the process of bringing economic and social development, or progressive betterment, of the current system will bring progress and things like hunger will disappear. If, however, the cause of poverty is seen as dialectical, that poverty is oppression and is the product of the economic organization of society, then poverty is seen as a collective and conflictive phenomenon. This phenomenon can only be overcome by replacing the present social system with an alternative one.[1]

The dialectical understanding and approach to poverty is consistent with the views of community development. Academic and practitioner Jim Ife, writing out of Curtin University in the 1990s, saw that in Western society community has effectively broken down to the point where it is not

---

1. Leonardo Boff and Clodovis Boff, *Introducing Liberation Theology*, (Kent, UK: Burns & Oats, 1987), 26-27.

a significant element of contemporary life. This has meant that the poor and marginalized have been cared for by human services, within a welfare model and not empowered through the context of community, which has previously been the case for centuries in traditional communities. Like the liberation theologian, Jim Ife believes that this system, and indeed society, needs to be transformed, and in fact he sees it necessary for our survival in the west.[2]

The second mediation is *hermeneutical*. In this mediation the liberation theologian looks at the whole problem through the lens of Scripture. First, recognizing the poor as the disfigured Son of God. It's easy to read over those words rather quickly and move on. But let's stop for a moment. What difference would it make if we truly saw the poor in our community as the disfigured Son of God? That they wear our scars, they are victims of a system that has promoted wealth for a few, sustainability (of sorts) for many, yet terrible soul crushing heartache for those at the bottom.

The theologian bears the weight of the sorrow and hopes of the poor, seeking to bring light and inspiration from the Scripture. The whole process becomes informed by Scripture, reminding the searcher that God is the father of life and advocate of the poor. As we know, the witness of Scripture tells of the prophecy of the new world, that the Kingdom is given to the poor, and the Church as sign and vehicle is to be a sharing Church. Again, some really confronting words and ideas. What does it mean for our local church community to be a sharing community? To give away what we have been given. Through the hermeneutic of the poor (using the poor as a key to understanding Scripture) an interpretation is arrived at that leads to inner change (conversion) and change in history (revolution).[3] Many Catholics see conversion as an ongoing process - that we continually need to turn away from the things of the world that would entice us, instead moving towards God and his Kingdom. Revolution here refers to change at the heart of the system, that then permeates throughout all of society. Whilst these are broad themes, liberation theology has a particular focus on contextualization, the answering of new questions posed by those contexts and essentially a new codification of the Christian mystery. In essence, interpreting Scripture, God's relationship to us and the world from where

---

2. Jim Ife, *Community Development: Creating community alternatives - vision, analysis and practice,* (Melbourne, VIC: Longman, 1995), 15.

3. Boff and Boff, *Introducing Liberation Theology,* 32-35.

we sit, in this case with the poor. The focus on God's work in the world as contextual and transformational is echoed by Wright. He understands that God is working and invites us to work with him towards a better future for the poor and marginalized in this world and sees this as central to God's mission.[4]

The third mediation is *practical*, and completes the circle, with a back to action focus. This action is seen as the work of love and manifests itself in a striving for justice. It works for the renewal of the Church and the transformation of society. The strategies and tactics favour non-violent methods, dialogue, persuasion, moral pressure and passive resistance, being true to the ethic of the gospel.[5] These are played out in micro actions on the macro system and lead to the design of a program for action. An example of a micro action can be seen in friends of mine who have been involved in the *Love Makes a Way* campaign discussed earlier, that has seen groups of Christians passively occupying the offices of politicians in an effort to raise attention to the plight of refugee children in detention centres. They simply arrive, sit in the reception area, pray and sometimes sing songs. At times they have been removed by police. Their actions, whilst seemingly small, are part of a force they hope will eventually change the system.

Key Themes of Liberation Theology

In order to make solid links between liberation theology and ABCD we need to not only understand the mediations outlined above, but the key themes that run through this brand of theology. As you read them take a few moments to think through how they apply to your setting and the changes that would occur if they were adopted. According to Boff and Boff there are nine key themes;

1. **Living and true faith includes the practice of liberation.** Proponents of liberation theology see that the divine reality penetrates every level of human history. Our faith helps us determine where in that history God was present and absent. In the light of faith, orthodoxy (right belief) is not enough, and needs to be made true in love, solidarity, hunger for justice, ultimately in orthopraxis (right action). Without action of this

---

4. Wright, *Surprised by Hope*, 204.
5. Boff and Boff, *Introducing Liberation Theology*, 40.

nature, faith is not authentic (Matt 25:35 and Jas 2:20-21).6

2. **The Living God sides with the oppressed against the pharaohs of this world.** Liberation theology seeks to bring out the characteristics of God that directly address the practice of liberation. God is beyond our understanding yet is not terrifying, but full of tenderness, particularly towards the oppressed (Exod 3:7-8). God is glorified in life sustaining activities and is worshipped through the doing of justice. This reflects his own nature as *goël* - doer of justice for the weak, comforter of orphans and widows. God is a social being and in this way, the Trinity is a model relationship of absolute equality and reciprocity. It is a prototype of what society should be. Affirming and respecting individuality, enabling persons to live in deep communion with each other. This ideal is of course very different to the world as it currently is. Our society is largely individualistic, and so does not reflect the mystery of the Holy Trinity. If it is to bear the image and likeness of the Trinity it needs to be transformed.[7]

3. **The Kingdom is God's project in history and eternity.** By revealing the Kingdom, liberation theologians understand that Jesus revealed God's divine plan. This is to be worked out through the course of history and constitutes God's future in eternity. When the Kingdom comes in its fullness there will be total liberation of all creation, purification from all oppressors. The Kingdom embraces all things, sacred and secular history, individuals and the cosmos. In different ways the Kingdom is present where people bring about justice, seek comradeship, forgive each other and promote life. This has particular expression in the Church which is the perceptible sign, privileged instrument, initial budding forth, core principle, liver of the gospel, blessed to be a blessing, and the body of Christ. As a universal project the Kingdom is the link between all these different factors. It encompasses creation, redemption, time and eternity.[8] Both Wright and Newbigin echo these beliefs in their understanding of Kingdom and God's work in the world.

4. **Jesus Son of God took on oppression in order to set us free.** Jesus is God in human form. As such he lived his life in a time in history,

---

6.   Boff and Boff, *Introducing Liberation Theology*, 49-50.

7.   Boff and Boff, *Introducing Liberation Theology*, 50-52.

8.   Boff and Boff, *Introducing Liberation Theology*, 52-53.

with all the cultural mores attached to that. His human life was marked by the contradictions left by sin, and of course his purpose in being incarnated was for the work of redemption. Jesus became a servant (Phil 2:6-11). His focus was the Kingdom and he taught that it was at hand. His first public word in Luke 4:16-21 laid out his program for social reform. He took on the hopes of the oppressed, recognizing that ultimately the Kingdom speaks of liberation from sin. This liberating presence is a present reality offered to all. The process of conversion, therefore, leads to a change of attitude that transforms all our interactions. This transformation is informed and guided by the beatitudes (Matt 5:2-12). Because of people's refusal to convert, the only way for Jesus to stay faithful to his own teaching and to the Father was martyrdom. The cross is the expression of the human rejection of Jesus and the acceptance of us by the Father, through sacrificing His son. The resurrection uncovers the meaning of the Kingdom - that life would be victorious and universal peace would be the fruit of divine justice. The resurrection showed full liberation from obstacles that stand in the way of the Lordship of God, and the full realization of all dynamic forces for life and glory placed by God in humans and the whole of creation. The resurrection also reveals the meaning of the death of the innocent (Jesus), rejected for having proclaimed a greater justice. Those unjustly put to death for a good cause share in Jesus' resurrection. Following Jesus means taking up His cause, and bearing the persecution it brings, in the hope of inheriting full liberation.[9]

5. **The Holy Spirit, Father of the poor, is present in the struggle of the oppressed.** The Spirit was sent into the world to further and complete the work of redemption and liberation. The Spirit is present in everything that implies movement, transformation and growth. No one is beyond the reach of the Spirit. He fills people with enthusiasm and special charisms to change religion and society, breaking open rigid institutions and making things new. The Spirit prevents us from forgetting eternity or succumbing to appeals of the flesh and empowers the poor to live and struggle, providing hope that united, the people will set themselves free. The Spirit is evidenced amongst the oppressed by piety, sense of God, solidarity, hospitality, fortitude, native wisdom, love for children, celebration, joy and serenity in the face of suffering.

9.   Boff and Boff, *Introducing Liberation Theology*, 53-55.

Because of the Holy Spirit the ideals of equality, fellowship, and hope for a world where it is easier to love and see God in the other become closer to tangible reality.[10]

6. **Mary is the prophetic and liberating woman of the people.** Originating in the Catholic world, liberation theology has a place for Mary. They see her as the Mother of God, holding her in greatness, because of her lowliness. Mary is the perfect example of faith and being available for God's purpose. She thinks of others. Like Mary, it is only possible to be liberators if we free ourselves from our own preoccupation and place our lives at the service of others. Mary also knew poverty, suffering, flight and exile (Matt 2:13-23).[11]

7. **The Church is the sign and instrument of liberation.** The Church is the inheritor of the mystery of Christ and His spirit, and is the organized human response to God's gift. In liberation theology the best mission is allowing the poor to become the Church, and allowing the Church to become a truly poor church and a church of the poor. Communion is the structural and structuring theological value of the Church. Rather than the Church being an institutional hierarchy, the structured Church needs to reflect the community of the faithful living in relationships of sharing, love and service. It is the embodiment of the meeting between faith and life, gospel and the signs of the time. The Church needs to have a sense of pilgrimage. Think here of our earlier discussions on liminality and communitas. If it is to be the people of God it first has to become a people, a network of living communities, working out understandings, planning action, organizing itself. In this way communities as a whole take on the task of evangelization. A church born of the faith of the people, shows itself as a sign of integral liberation and an instrument for its implementation.[12] Right here we clearly see a mandate for the Church to be involved in community change. Remember too our earlier conversation about the nature of the Church. Liberation theology clearly points us towards an authentic expression of the faith, with the poor as a guiding lens for our interpretation of Scripture and our action in the world.

---

10. Boff and Boff, *Introducing Liberation Theology,* 55-56.
11. Boff and Boff, *Introducing Liberation Theology,* 56-58.
12. Boff and Boff, *Introducing Liberation Theology,* 59-60.

8. **The rights of the poor are God's rights.** Theological reflection on the primacy of the dignity of the poor heightened part of the Catholic Church's concern for and defence of human rights. Individualism has seen a lessening of human rights, over and against the benefiting of society and solidarity. Liberation theology brings a corrective, using biblical sources to show God's heart for the poor. There is a developed hierarchy of rights, forming a mode of operandi: one, life and the means to sustain it, that is, food, work, basic health care, housing, literacy; two, the freedom of expression, conscience, movement and religion.[13]

9. **Liberated human potential becomes liberative.** Liberation theologians believe sin festers in the institutions and structures that act contrary to God's purposes. They understand structures to be forms of relatedness between things and the people caught up in them. Overcoming social sin requires the will to transform structures, allowing for more justice and participation. Social sin is to be overcome by social grace, the fruit of God's gift and human endeavour, which is inspired by God. Love is seen as collaboration in the forming of new structures, supporting those campaigning for a better quality of life, essentially a political commitment to the poor. Those that do not support Jesus' ethic need to be opposed. Unequal and unjust relationships need to be tackled. However, in that opposition the challenge is to respect different opinions, to love, not to be deceived by emotions, and to safeguard the unity of the community. In this way persecution and martyrdom is to be expected. The follower can only sustain this intense involvement with the life of the poor by being truly free, a member of the Kingdom of God. This reflects the death and resurrection of Christ. Liberative Christians unite heaven and earth, building the human city with the eschatological city of God. The task is to do everything towards full liberation and when the Lord comes, he will bring it to completion.[14]

Reflections and Connections

I wonder how you find yourself responding to the key themes running through liberation theology. For me personally, after spending over twenty years working with marginalized people and seeking to bring change to communities, I find it refreshing, life giving and affirming. At times my

---

13. Boff and Boff, *Introducing Liberation Theology,* 60-61.
14. Boff and Boff, *Introducing Liberation Theology,* 61-63.

journey in these things has brought me into conflict with those holding a more traditional theology. These conflicts have often been personally damaging, yet in some small way reminds me of the importance of following Jesus to stand with the poor and to embrace suffering for that stand. This is not unusual through, with liberation theology being opposed both within sections of the Catholic and Protestant Churches. The Vatican saw that it used Marxist concepts and associated the hierarchy of the Catholic Church in South America with the oppressors of the people (i.e. as part of the problem).[15] Other opposition included its focus on systemic sin almost to the exclusion of individual offenders. Newbigin also challenged the theology's focus on the overthrowing of the oppressor, believing that in human nature, as a new group rises to power they too will become oppressors.[16] Unfortunately this is a real danger as recent events in South Africa have shown. Without going into a lot of detail, the ruling party, the ANC, the one that formerly struggled to unite a people to overcome apartheid are now being accused of injustices, particularly over spending. The intoxication of power and wealth is at times overwhelming and is something we all need to be mindful of.

Again for me personally, as a Christian community activist, this theology is authentic and provides a clear link between theory and action. Whilst not adopting all the Catholic nuances, it essentially maintains an orthodox understanding of the role of Christ, the Trinity, the special place of the poor in God's heart, the Kingdom as God's project and the place of the Church, of course with a higher focus on its role as liberator. The points of difference hone this theology towards orthopraxis, right action, and not just right thinking. Liberation theology sees that faith has to be lived out for it to be authentic, most notably in the liberation of the poor.

Liberation theology can have a tendency to feel combative, with a focus of the ending of oppression, rather than the empowerment of community, as would be true for community development. However it is important to remember that the aim is for the poor to rise and take their place. With this in mind the theology and connected process becomes ultimately empowering and allows for community self-determination.

---

15. Michael Novak, *Will It Liberate: Questions About Liberation Theology,* (New York, NY: Paulist, 1986), 66-67.

16. Newbigin, *The Gospel in a Pluralist Society,* 151.

Added to this, the Holy Spirit is the forerunner of liberation, motivating and shaping it to reflect Jesus' ethic. The theology points to God's heart for and defence of the poor, going as far as to say it is the poor that makes up his primary concern. Another point of difference between mainstream and liberation theology, and a clear connector with community development, is the understanding of social grace and social sin. Community Development would not understand society in these terms. However, it works to empower whole marginalized communities to overcome issues and structures that are in effect disempowering. Community Development, with liberation theology, longs for a world where people have their basic needs met and the individual can live out their life and purpose mindful of and in the context of community.

Liberation theology plays the part of a bridge between theology and action. On the other side of that bridge are our communities and practices such as Appreciative Inquiry, which we explored in the opening pages of this book, and Asset Based Community Development, which is essentially an approach to working with communities that seeks to unearth and promote the strengths already present in a community. This line of thinking and practice fits very well with sentiments expressed by leaders of the ANC in their struggle towards equality (which by the way is nowhere near complete) 'nothing for us without us.' This sentiment has been echoed by Melbourne based community activists Experts by Experience (EXE). The group consists of people who have experienced homelessness and marginalization firsthand and are passionate about creating a more just society. Like ABCD the idea behind this statement is that everyone has something to bring to the task of community change.

Asset Based Community Development (ABCD)

Put simply, ABCD is a process for the empowerment of whole communities through the utilizing of strengths within that community.[17] The founders of the methodology, John Kretzman and John McKnight, see this as a means of sustainable development. The concept of sustainability is becoming more and more important as we face the rising costs of welfare, the effects of global warming on the planet, growth in the population and number of cities around the globe, and the dangers of individualism and consumerism

---

17. John P. Kretzman and John L. McKnight, *Building Communities from the Inside Out: A Path Toward Finding and Mobilizing a Community's Assets* (Chicago, IL: ACTA, 1993), 1.

and numerous other concerns that threaten individual and community wellbeing. Associated with sustainable development are questions raised by the UNHCR around people who are just on the edges of poverty, perhaps having moved through it or close to experiencing it. What will it take for them to increase their resilience so poverty is not experienced, either for the first time or as a recurring phenomenon?

Community development in a Western context is a relatively new concept. Traditionally it has been associated with communities in the developing world. However, with the lessening of social capital within communities, the rise of individualism, increased personal mobility, longer work hours and the increasing divide between the rich and poor, even within the same local area, there is an increasing need to focus on the restructuring and rebuilding of community in our Western context.

ABCD recognizes and values the contribution of three levels within community. First, the gift of individuals. Kretzman and McKnight emphasize that everyone within a community has something to offer to build it up. They especially include the physically and mentally handicapped and those marginalized in other ways. They advocate for an intensive mapping exercise that includes the interviewing of individuals and the creation of a skills registry, indicating what people are willing to offer into the community.[18] The next level of contribution, in the United States, is called citizen associations. These include churches, clubs, cultural groups, essentially where people come together around a particular purpose, sport or hobby. In Australia this would include many smaller not-for-profit organizations. Kretzman and McKnight believe that the associational life within any community is usually underestimated. Quite often these groups can be stretched past their original purpose to become full contributors to the development process.[19]

Formal institutions comprise the third level of community. These include businesses, schools, libraries, hospitals, local councils and various social service organizations. These institutions make up the most visible aspects of the community's fabric. Enlisting them in the community development

---

18. Kretzman and McKnight, *Building Communities from the Inside Out*, 6-7.

19. Kretzman and McKnight, *Building Communities from the Inside Out*, 6.
I believe this statement needs to be tested in an Australian context, and in fact might be found to be more true in disadvantaged communities.

process is essential to its success. Whilst it is relatively simple to list what they bring to the community, through funding requirements and other restrictions it can be difficult to encourage them to fully participate in the process. However, inevitably there are people of goodwill within those institutions who can help broker partnerships and connections, perhaps even to the extent of letting the community control how the relationship works between the entity and the community development process.[20]

Five steps towards whole community mobilization

Kretzman and McKnight have developed a five step process that outlines how a whole community can be mobilized to better meet its own needs. This is the type of process that a church, with a robust Kingdom theology and a shape that allows it to engage in mission as an open generous association, could facilitate. Once again as you read through the process, imagine what this would be like in your context.

Step One: Creating an Asset Map.

An asset map is a way of documenting the strengths unearthed in a local community and can form the essential step of research. As mentioned earlier so many social service organizations, including churches launch projects and programs are quite ignorant of the local community and their aspirations. If you are considering embarking on creating an asset map, this type of research blends well with Appreciative Inquiry (AI). Put simply, AI asks questions such as the following:

- What do you enjoy about living in your community?
- What is working well here?
- What would you like to see happen over the next five years?

As you work firstly with individuals to unearth their skills and interests, ABCD or strength based questions include:

- What arc some things that you enjoy doing?
- What are some of the skills you have?
- Are there skills you have that would be good enough that others would hire you to do them?
- Are there any skills you would like to teach others?

---

20. Kretzman and McKnight, *Building Communities from the Inside Out*, 346.

For people who have been experiencing long-term poverty, unemployment or other forms of marginalization, even being asked these questions can begin empowerment and even liberation.

Secondly, begin to map community organizations, including churches, clubs and not-for-profits. It would be helpful to go and visit these groups and begin to form relationships with them. As you meet with them include the AI approach in your list of questions, beginning to gain their perspective on the local community. It's also important that you work to understand them and their interests and objective in and for the community. Ask them also what they believe they might be able to bring to a community renewal project. This will help you map their strengths and contributions as an organization.

The third part of the asset map is perhaps the most difficult - working with established institutions. As mentioned they are often limited in their ability to contribute but because of their size and the resources they already supply to the community, they are an essential part of the ABCD process. Look for the people of goodwill within the institution who may be able to leverage relationships and resources. Again connect with the AI questions and then explore their aspirations for the community and the strengths they bring to those aspirations.

As you compile your findings into a single document there are a few things to note:

- First, your work with the asset map is not complete. It is a living document that will morph and change over time as the community ebbs and flows, and it is important to review it regularly and keep it updated.

- It is quite a task to document the skills of a whole community and it will be important not to become overwhelmed. It's easier to start with those you are already connected with and bring in others as you can. Alternatively if you have a particular target group in mind, seek out willing people from that community to be the first ones in your growing asset map.

- The people you meet and build relationships with in the research phase can become willing partners in the project moving forward.

- The data you are gathering, remembering privacy considerations, is a resource in and of itself and you might like to consider releasing your research document as a way of highlighting the work that is going on in the community, cementing relationships and providing a tool for other organizations.

Research was the first step that I did as Amy and I started Big House Communities in the Outer South East of Melbourne. At the time I wasn't aware of AI and ABCD. However, the questions I used were congruent with these approaches. It was hard work, yet a wonderful experience to meet community members, in their homes, at the shopping centre, wherever they were. I also enjoyed immensely meeting people from the social services, schools, local council and other organizations, who were to become close allies in the task of community change. Unfortunately some of my most difficult encounters were with leaders of other churches. We were new to the community and so understandably they were skeptical about who we were as well as our approach that was radically different to theirs. I'm pleased to say a couple of the ministers became good friends, while others held us at arms' length throughout all of Big House Communities' life.

After the research phase I compiled a document that we publicly launched. Because I went with the approach of a learner and someone who wanted to contribute to the community I found many open doors and began relationships that blossomed into significant working partnerships as together we sought to impact the community. Releasing the document also built our credibility as an organization, because we delivered on our promise of delivering a document and it was of a high enough quality that it was used by other organizations as reading material for their boards and reference points for grant applications.

The asset map then becomes a reference point from which to ask, what resources does this community have to solve its own issues?

Step Two: Building Relationships.

This is a core element in successful community development and indeed a key to living a successful life. There have been many books on the topic and lots of theories ruminated, however I want to expand on this essential ingredient to ABCD, taking it beyond the individual to the community.

Can I encourage you to stop and think with me for a moment about your local community where you live or work? How strong is the relational web? By relational web I mean the connections between different entities or even people in that community. A related question: what are the elements that make up that web or community? Sometimes it's hard to stop and analyze the waters that we swim in or the air we breathe. In each of our communities there will be elements that seek to meet the needs we have, whether they present as physical, emotional or spiritual. As we explored in the asset map, they include the business community, schools, medical care, friends and family, sporting and other clubs, churches and the religious expressions of other faith communities, libraries, local government, social services, media outlets and so on. If these elements of the community are working well and in harmony, they form *an interconnected web of relationships, structures and institutions, where people can gain a sense of belonging and support to discover and live out their place and purpose as contributors in the world.*[21] If you like, a safety net of relationships has been established which affords the individual the opportunity to explore more of their external and internal worlds. There may even be the opportunity to explore new abilities in this context.

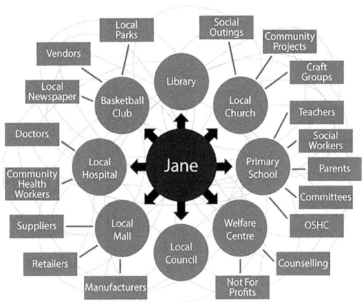

Jane's Community. The ideal community recognizes the individual and places them in a relational web, which provides for their physical, emotional and spiritual needs and those of their family.

21.   Working definition of a community, developed and taught by Andre Van Eymeren.

Unfortunately we know only too well that our communities aren't like that and in fact the relational web that provides this safety is broken in so many places. The causes of this rupture are numerous, including individualism, consumerism, family breakdown, domestic violence, tall poppy syndrome, selfishness, addictions of various types... And the list goes on. The results are equally as devastating both for individual psyches and communities more generally.

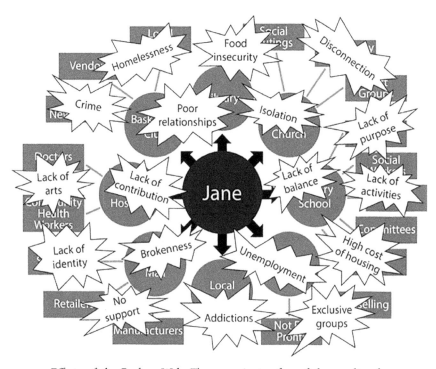

Effects of the Broken Web. These are just a few of the results of a broken relational web. As we look at our communities the story is way too familiar.

Even within a household the relational web can be broken, leaving the members floating and feeling disconnected from each other and broader society. Some would argue if the basic building block of a community is broken, i.e. the household, there is no point looking to a more utopian hope for our communities. Sociologist Jim Ife believes that we must start with this utopian view, as it provides inspiration and a framework for development that moves us from reaction to a focus on medium to long-term goals.[22] As we've explored previously, this thinking is echoed by the prophet Isaiah as he outlines what a community could look like. He sees a place where there is joy, the young and old are valued, each have what they need in terms of shelter and food, there is a strong connection between work and purpose, and the people recognize their dependence on God (Isa 65:17-25). The core building block for this type of world is relational local communities.[23]

Rebuilding the Relational Web – Creating Relational Proximity

Many of us tend to give airplay to the fact that relationships are important yet so often we behave in a way that betrays this understanding. I suspect part of the reason for this is the intangible nature of relating to others. As we think about relationships in the context of community, there is the internal

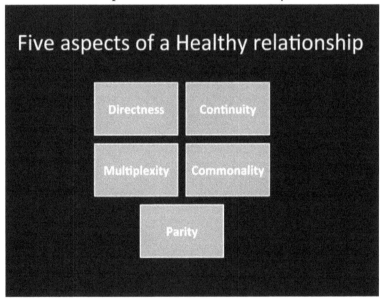

relationship that we have with ourselves, the inter-personal relationships and then our interaction with the broader social fabric. Added to this there

---

22. Jim Ife, *Community Development*, 98.

23. The diagrams and associated text first appeared as a Conference paper presented at *Urban Life Together: Inhabiting Our Neighbourhoods,* October 17-18, 2014, Urban Seed. Published online November 12, 2015. The full paper can be viewed at http://www.urbanseed. org/publications/articles/2015/11/12/andre-van-eymeren-relating-for-gold.

are the relationships we have within our organizations and the relationships those organizations have with partners and other stakeholders. The Relational Proximity Framework, designed by Michael Schluter and the team at the Jubilee Centre, gives us the tools to understand the complexities of these relationships and what is going wrong when they feel like they are falling apart.

Put simply, The Relational Proximity Framework consists of the five dimensions or levers of a relationship: directness, continuity, multiplexity, commonality and parity. They relate to the domains of a relationship and they have a felt outcome.[24] The following is a little subjective as we explore the experience of the relationship in terms of the type of relationship. The levels of each dimension vary and would be different in a spouse relationship compared with a business one.

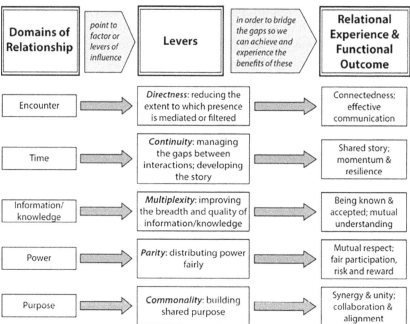

Image produced by Jubilee Centre depicting The Relational Proximity Framework. See footnote 26.

As we go through the five dimensions think about them in terms of one of your significant relationships.

24. Various in-house training modules, the concept first appeared in Michael Schluter & David Lee, *The R Factor,* (London: Hodder & Stoughton Religious, 1993).

Directness refers to the amount and types of contact. It asks questions such as, is the time we spend connecting enough? Directness also explores the mode of communication; face to face, phone, email. Today email is fast becoming core to the way we relate, however what is left out when face to face contact goes missing?

Continuity is about shared story or history over time. A few years ago I saw my cousin for the first time in ten years. During our later teen years we had a close relationship, often spending the weekends at each other's place. We then both got married and our paths separated. When we reconnected, after some momentary awkwardness, we picked up right where we left off. Other relationships aren't like this. My high school graduating year is organizing a 25 year reunion. I haven't seen or had contact with most of the people in my year over those 25 years… awkward! Continuity looks at foundation or history. Have there been time gaps in the relationship's development? It also looks to the future. Do you anticipate a positive future or are the difficulties going to swamp the connection? A sense of belonging is also important for continuity. Belonging is often fostered through genuine welcome and shared tasks where the other knows that their contribution is seen and valued. Other questions that bring continuity to light include, do both parties have loyalty to the relationship? Do they hold the relationship at the same level of importance?

Multiplexity refers to the breadth and depth of knowledge that you possess about the other person. Do you know how they will respond in different circumstances and why? What do you know about their background and their culture? What do you know about their skills, interests and talents? Gaining this sort of knowledge about the other person presumes a level of trust and openness to each other and so multiplexity is also concerned with appreciation. Does each party feel known and appreciated by the other?

Every month I catch up with two other guys to talk about life's journey and how we are responding to that journey. Although we don't see each other all that often in between, we each know a lot about each other's lives and can input into situations they are facing with a high degree of accuracy. We have spent the time and made the choice to develop the trust that allows us the freedom to be open and honest with each other.

Parity is to do with the distribution of power in a relationship. As we think about working with marginalized communities, parity is very important to consider. When a trained social or community worker, or even someone volunteering with a church welfare program, is connecting with a client or participant the power tends to be all in the workers favor. These encounters can tend to be very disempowering for those for whom we are seeking to make a difference. Thinking about your significant relationship, can each person take action without fear of being told off? Are you consulted, heard? Can you influence the relationship? Can the other person?

The perception of fairness is also very important. Is it fair that a job network provider can decide whether someone is entitled to their Centrelink benefits or not? Is there excessive power from one side? Are the risks and rewards shared fairly in the relationship? Respect is key. Is each party valued by the other, for who they are and what they have to offer?

The relationship between CEO and board is always interesting. As a CEO I was working on a project with a board member and I found my frustration levels increasing. We stopped and took the time to talk it through. I felt that the parity was out because I perceived I was taking the time and financial risk and if things went south the fallout would affect me more. On talking it through I realized the board member was making considerable sacrifice to be a part of the project and in fact we were both equally committed to its outcome.

For those entrenched in some kind of poverty this question is key. There are a couple of dynamics at work. First, some people on welfare have an entitlement mentality, that they have a right to a certain type of help. This attitude can ultimately disempower the carer and the one being helped. The other dynamic can be one of victim, which can lead to all the power being in the hands of the receiver.

Commonality looks to the future. Are there shared goals? What will get in the way of achieving them? Is there enough common purpose to overcome the difficulties? Does each party have similar commitment to the goals? Does your connection go beyond achieving the goals? Is the energy created greater than the sum of the parts? Do you have a convergence of values and spirit that almost doesn't need a goal? Essentially commonality asks, what does the future look like? Is there a shared path towards it? Many married couples can struggle once the kids leave home and commonality can be a part of that struggle. When the kids are at home the common goals are often around raising the family and making sure they are safe and well cared for. As this role changes couples can find it difficult to re-orientate to a shared future outside the kids.

In the helping relationship commonality can also be an issue. What is the appropriate level of investment for me as a worker in the goals of a friend from the street?

The Relational Proximity Framework is a helpful way to think about our relationships, including our 'helping' relationships and check in to make sure our connection with others is empowering them to move forward, not leaving them frustrated and feeling unheard.

Putting this back into the context of ABCD, every time a community member is linked with others for problem solving purposes, or an association links with an institution, the community is strengthened and becomes more self-reliant. This is particularly true when a marginalized person or 'stranger' is connected into the process. Kretzman and McKnight have found that as communities engage in relationship building in this way, people more readily come to believe they are capable of acting as effective problem solvers. They slowly begin to look to internal capacities, before looking to outside help.[25]

Step Three: Mobilizing for economic development and information sharing.

If I'm being honest this is the part of the strategy that I struggle with, if only a little. Not so much the communication but the generation of economic development. I have very little skills in developing my own personal finances let alone that of a community. Putting my insecurities aside, there are many communities that are economically depressed, for reasons such as high unemployment, local skills not matching industry needs and local economic assets not being mobilized. As part of your asset map it will be important to note the skills of local residents that can be used for economic development. This can happen at two levels, firstly generating finances for themselves through micro-enterprises and secondly using skills to generate income and change in the community.

The Broadway United Methodist Church in Indianapolis employed a community worker at least in part for this purpose. In an effort to adopt a more empowering approach to work in their community they stopped all

---

25. Kretzman and McKnight, *Building Communities from the Inside Out*, 346.

their welfare programs and shifted there focus to an ABCD based approach. The community worker was actually employed to be a community listener. His job was to go and meet different people in the community, encouraging them to pursue the development of their skills and dreams as well as looking to connect people of like minds. This approach began to change the community and the role of the church within it. During the week the church building now resembles a business hub with a whole bunch of enterprises and initiatives using space. In addition there are numerous gatherings around the community to dream, plan and collaborate.[26]

As well, local associations and institutions need to be urged to contribute to the local economy, particularly sourcing as much as they can locally. Whilst not subscribing to every aspect of 'localism' as a political philosophy and economic strategy, it has something of merit to offer to the conversation around the development of relational communities.[27] As its name suggests, localism prioritizes the local. It supports local production and consumption of goods, local control of government, production of local history, culture and the forming of a local identity. If the connection between these elements were strengthened in any local community, the broken relational web would begin to heal. Overall the aim is to help communities decrease imports, become more self-sustaining and increase the export of local products.[28]

When it comes to strengthening the economy of a local community, Peter Kenyon is perhaps one of Australia's leading proponents, working in line with and promoting ABCD principles. With his people-focused approach he has spent most of the last twenty years travelling around Australia and internationally sharing practical ways to do this. His website bankofideas.com.au is full of resources, many of which he calls *copyleft*, meaning that they are free to use for any group that wants to work to strengthen their community.

The other part to this step is to do with communication. When people lived in a village, the village well or square was a key hub of the community.

---

26. Robert King, "Death and Resurrection of an Urban Church," *Faith and Leadership*, accessed November 2015, https://www.faithandleadership.com/death-and-resurrection-urban-church.

27. Oliver Hartwich, *A Global Perspective on Localism*, (Hamilton, NZ: The New Zealand Initiative and LGNZ, 2013).

28. Jane Jacobs cited in Kretzman and McKnight, *Building Communities from the Inside Out*, 350.

It was the place people gathered and shared information. However, our communication is a bit more scattered today. As people concerned about community development, we will want to have a clear understanding of the modes of communication, including the 'grapevine' within a community as well as what is being communicated. Modes of communication vary from the formal, including local papers, radio and newsletters, to informal modes or the grapevine.

During my time working with Big House in Pakenham, we used both formal and informal communication. Whenever we were about to launch a new project, I would connect with the local papers both through a press release and on the phone. They would then usually send a photographer to document the project as well as print, quite often word for word, the press release. However, although it was in transition, 'old Pakenham' still operated a bit like a country town, in that the grapevine was very important. One of the key nodes of the vine was the local barber and former football coach. He was a third or fourth generation barber and many of the older men of the town would go for a 'haircut' (even though they barely had any hair), just to sit in his shop and shoot the breeze. So if you were able to get the barber enthused about your project, he would be better than the best PR money could buy.

Think about how communication works in your community, and there are many ways. I've even heard of a new housing estate establishing a kind of intranet portal where people who had not yet begun moving into the area could begin to build relationships with each other. As you use the different modes of communication it will be important to think about your audience and match your communication to their needs.

Step Four: Convening the community to develop a vision and a plan.

Let me paint a picture of where the ABCD process is up to. The asset map has been developed and is continually updated. This has given the facilitation group a good picture of the strengths of the local community. People are beginning to use their skills and gifts to start micro-enterprises as well as being encouraged to see how they may contribute to the larger picture. Relationships have been forming between people of like minds. A group interested in community gardening may have formed, or a group has gotten together to clean up a local park or put on an event aimed at drawing people together. Networks have also been strengthened between different organizations and institutions. There is a pride forming in the local community as people are encouraged to buy local and appreciate the skills and products from within their own community. Communication is also happening effectively and people are beginning to get on board with projects that they are interested in. Slowly the community is taking on a new positive vibe.

It's now time to begin drawing the different energies together to think about the community as a whole; to dream together about what the community could look like in five years, or three, then begin to plan towards it.

Invercargill in New Zealand is a community who has done just that. South Alive was established through a small steering group who held a community meeting in 2012. It then became a charitable organization and a hub for community rejuvenation. The group formed its vision. They wanted Invercargill to become 'a vibrant and diverse community that takes the lead in its own future.' The way they are achieving that is through their mission: 'empowered by our strengths as a community, we will build a place to live and work that engenders pride and inspires us.' Since that community meeting they have developed a diverse range of teams who work on various projects including children and youth, creating stronger neighborhoods, arts, housing, beautification, fruit and nut trees, marketing and events and a dog park. Their website, as well as serving the needs of the organization and promoting what they are doing, provides a hub for local information and story telling.[29]

Another example of a community that has come together with some remarkable results is Grand Crossing, Chicago.[30] Under the leadership of Theaster Gates, who describes himself as a humble potter, the community has revitalized disused houses and buildings, turning them into community assets used as spaces for generating creativity, community gatherings to remember and become inspired, as well as a listening and learning hub. Again it was a process of bringing like-minded people together to dream, to plan and begin to take action towards change.

---

29. For more stories and ideas visit South Alive's website, http://www.southalive.org.nz/.

30. Theaster Gates, "How to Revive a Neighbourhood with Imagination, Beauty and Art," *TED*, March 2015, accessed March 2016, https://www.ted.com/talks/theaster_gates_how_to_revive_a_neighborhood_with_imagination_beauty_and_art?language=en.

So again, once the energies in a local community have been harnessed, they need to be directed. Identity, values and vision need to be shared. Without a common understanding of these things, the work of regeneration is very difficult to sustain. Community planning can be used to set the tone for the entire regeneration process, working to mobilize local assets and capacity. Beginning with the recognizable assets, it is important to invite those to the table that are not normally seen as community leaders. This includes young people, people experiencing homelessness, or those with a disability. Other people not often included in the planning table could be small business owners, stay at home mums and so on. It is also important to include people representing associations and institutions. With a rich and diverse planning table, it is easier to see the wealth of local resources that can be used to creatively solve local community issues from within. Whilst the vision and mission for the community can have a longer projection, the effective planning process needs to be tied to problem solving. This will help it to be grounded and not too future orientated.[31]

Wyndham City Council in the west of Melbourne provided a helpful blend of the long and medium term in their recent 2040 consultations. They were aware that change, particularly around infrastructure, can take a long time to implement, so they asked their community to help them shape a twenty-five year vision of what the growing community could look like. One of the delightful aspects of this process was the video stories collected from residents. These stories told of diverse experiences of the City of Wyndham. As well, they pointed toward individual and community aspirations. Setting this as the context through a series of regional meetings, they unearthed many of the strengths of the community, as well as their medium term (four year) aspirations. Collating this data, the council was able to create meaningful, region based development plans.

Step Five: Leveraging outside resources to support locally driven development.

Unfortunately, due to a defective welfare system that leaves people and communities disempowered, many individuals and communities have developed a hand-out mentality. You may even have fallen victim to it yourself. Have you ever thought or uttered the words, 'they should fix that?' Who are 'they'? I remember hearing the story of an Eyre Peninsular

---

31. Kretzman and McKnight, *Building Communities from the Inside Out*, 352.

(South Australia) member of Federal Parliament, who was visiting a small community of her constituents. The community meeting she was attending was to discuss the possibility of an airstrip for the town. She was upfront and honest with the group who were initially looking for government help, stating that simply there would be no funding for a small rural community to build an airstrip. Instead of taking a defeatist attitude, someone said they had a grader, another person a bulldozer, a third offered other supplies and pretty soon they had everything they needed to build the airstrip and they did it themselves.

However it is not likely that a community will be able to muster all the resources needed to solve all its issues, and will need to enlist outside partners. Notice though how the language changes, instead of settling for the 'they should fix it' attitude the community has become proactive and is beginning to look for partners to meet their skill gaps. An important part of the empowerment and rejuvenation process is to first exhaust all the avenues of tackling an issue from within the community.

Is this Actually Possible?

This chapter started with a focus on Isaiah 58 and 65, which both paint a picture of the world God longs to see. What I have sought to do is outline a pathway towards such a world. Some would argue that this vision is utopian and not achievable. Ultimately it will only be fulfilled when God brings heaven to earth. However, it is the promise of this fulfilment and the beginning of its actualization in the here and now that motivates the Christian community development worker. As alluded to earlier, Jim Ife sees the utopian vision as essential for inspiration as well as providing a framework for the development of medium to long-term goals. So don't be afraid to hold onto passages like those in Isaiah that inspire you to action. A broad vision also allows room for problem solving that moves beyond reaction and is outside of the usual paradigm.[32]

Jim Ife argues that any community initiative that would emerge from a process like what is described above, needs to be run through a framework that embraces ecological sustainability and social justice. For people of faith, the Scriptures show God's concern for both. Whilst ecology and social justice relate to a desire to build the community, they have traditionally come from what could be seen as competing agendas. In the 1980s and 1990s

---

32. Ife, *Community Development*, 98.

social justice proponents wanted to see the community grown through job creation, but were not too concerned about the ecological impact. As too for those focused on ecology, they were concerned for long-term eco-sustainability, but not so concerned about the impact on the economy. Both these concerns could be seen in the debates over the damming of the Franklin River in Tasmania, and of course ongoing logging in that state.

When it comes to community development, Jim Ife sees the integration of these two important foci will ensure equitable and sustainable futures for communities. Each perspective is seeking a better world and encompasses a critique of the dominant social and political order. Both perspectives draw on the same intellectual traditions such as feminism, socialism and anarchism. Added to this, proponents of each position largely agree with the premise of the other, even if only superficially. This leaves space for effective collaboration, and integrated change strategies.[33] Put simply, as you begin to meet with others in your community you will notice people holding these different concerns. If you, as someone dedicated to bringing the whole community together, can recognize these concerns as valid and create room for them to be addressed, a harmony will develop around the planning table.

An example of this concept is social sustainability. Coming from a green perspective, it asks if a particular solution to a community or systemic issue is sustainable. It asks this question in terms of its impact on the social aspect of the community, as well as on the local economy, impact on families and on the environment. This way of thinking is a step towards holism. The Church has not been good at embracing this concept, despite being part of a Kingdom that embraces all of life. Holism requires the breaking down of dualisms including mind/body, knowledge/action (reflective of the thinking coming from liberation theology), fact/value (echoes of Newbigin's work, highlighting that the advances in science have been as big a faith leap as faith in Christ. Newbigin also focused on plausibility structures which reflect the values of society), and physical/social infrastructure.[34] As we've been discussing throughout this book such an approach requires a broadening of the knowledge base of most congregations and would require the Church to integrate theology with a range of other disciplines such as sociology,

---

33. Ife, *Community Development*, 83.

34. Ife, *Community Development*, 85. Author's own additions in parentheses.

ecology and economics. Helpfully, in some circles this thinking is already happening, but it needs to become more widespread.

This is the work of making connections, so key to successful community development. Connections not just between people, but between different issues and potential 'out of the box' solutions. Jim Ife understands that our society is very linear and not good at making connections, which in part has been a contributing factor to the breakdown of community and the failing of various social policies.[35] In addition to this our communities, cities and society generally have been developed in silos. This is very evident in local government where it is often difficult to get different parts of the organization to talk with each other.

Pleasingly, the City of Melbourne is tackling this issue, particularly around homelessness. They are forming relationships between community services and the operations team, that is, street cleaners, rubbish removal workers and others. These relationships particularly help in keeping track of rough sleepers. These types of connections need to expand outside a single organization, and go beyond issues of rough sleepers. A few years ago two colleagues and I came up with a concept we called synergistic dialogue, which aims to create a diverse planning table comprised of people coming from different perspectives all to tackle a single issue. In our case we were exploring the social environment for young people, and in particular youth suicide. I don't think we pushed the concept of synergistic dialogue to its extreme, but we were able to come up with some dynamic ideas for tackling the issue.

Taking all these things into consideration, the task of community development is to provide a framework for these physical and analytical connections and to help in the bringing of a new order. For those of us operating from a faith base, this new order needs to be in line with the values we see operating in God's Kingdom.

Reflection Questions

1. Explore your reaction to Liberation Theology as a theology of engagement? What is its most helpful aspect?

2. Asset Based Community Development or a strength-based

---

35. Ife, *Community Development*, 85.

approach to engagement is essential for empowering people to individually flourish and contribute to their communities. Why?

3. Relationships are a key part of this methodology. Spend some time thinking about the characteristics of a healthy relationship (directness, continuity, multiplexity, parity and commonality). As a result, which relationships in your life need work? What are the strengths and weaknesses of your church's or organization's relationship with those you are trying to help?

4. What steps will you take to begin working on ABCD in your community?

Chapter 8. - Working in Local Communities

The Spirit of Christ is the spirit of missions. The nearer we get to him, the more intensely missionary we become.

Henry Martyn

So far we have explored a little of Australian, and by circumspect Western culture, seeking for an understanding of what God is doing in the world. Through seeing God's Kingdom as present with us now and concerned about all of life and making it better now, we have seen that community development fits within a biblical mandate and as such churches are able to engage with it as a valid form of mission and not just something that is carried out in an overseas context. In addition, understanding community development as a valid form of mission allows us to form robust partnerships with others in our communities who are working along similar lines. In fact if we have the eyes to see, wherever we recognize the values of God's kingdom, it is present.

As a response we have explored the internal characteristics needed for a church to effectively engage with its community and have placed local communities in a broader postmodern context, tracking the development of thought from enchantment to disenchantment, through to re-enchantment. Liberation theology has been used as a bridge to Asset Based Community Development, a methodology that is congruent with a Kingdom understanding of local communities.

In this final chapter I would like to outline a few important aspects necessary for us to travel well on the journey towards effective community engagement. These centre around our own spiritual journey, a recovery of a missional imagination and a starting place.

Spirituality and the Missional Journey

Throughout this book I've alluded to my own journey which of course has led to my understanding of what God is doing in the world. It has been helpful over the last few years to reflect on that journey, beginning to see the stresses and strains of an unsustainable way of doing mission and life. I often describe myself as a recovering workaholic but perhaps its better to say that I am a recovering 'over-activist.' By that I mean there was a lack of balance in my approach to life and mission (truth be told, there probably still is, but I'm learning). When people would ask me what I was up to and I would go through the list, they would comment, 'gee, you're busy'. A successful day was one in which I felt like I produced what I set out to. It wasn't so much measured by the joy I brought to someone, or the listening I did to people's issues, although I think there were elements of these things present. It was what I sensed I achieved. Into this mix there was also the love of the new, the compelling fresh project or idea to pursue that sometimes meant existing projects did not get finished or did not reach their potential.

All this was fuelled by a big dream of changing the world, which I think - just on the quiet - was predominantly tied to ego. Now, I'm not trying to be hard on myself. I was truly and, I believe, continue to be, as faithful to God's call as I know how. It was just a little muddy, with lots of mixed motivations. Of course we will never reach true altruism, but growing in self-awareness and authenticity is an important part of the discipleship journey. I hasten to point out that none of what I described above is wrong in and of itself. If you have big dreams to change the world and are compelled by ideas and new projects, that is good. But check in to make sure those dreams are truly yours and they are located in the depth of who you are, deeper than ego, deeper than the 'should', even deeper than aspirations to live the 'big life'.

A book that has been important for me on the journey towards authenticity, is Parker Palmer' *Let Your Life Speak*. He talks about uncovering the true self and living life or experiencing our vocation from there.

> From the beginning, our lives lay down clues to selfhood and vocation, though the clues may be hard to decode. But trying to interpret them is profoundly worthwhile – especially when we are in our twenties or thirties or forties, feeling profoundly lost, having wandered, or been dragged, far away from our birthright gifts.[1]

In another passage Palmer makes a connection between this and his own journey:

> What I learnt about vocation is how one's values can do battle with one's heart. I felt morally compelled to work on the urban crisis, but doing so went against a growing sense that teaching might be my vocation. My heart wanted to keep teaching, but my ethics - laced liberally with ego –

---

1.   Parker Palmer, *Let Your Life Speak: Listening for the voice of vocation*, (CA, John Wiley & Sons, 2000), 15.

told me I was supposed to save the city.[2]

He goes on to explain that he got an opportunity to teach and take students out into the field. As he was doing this he realized that even as a community organizer he had been teaching, just in a classroom without walls: 'In fact, I could have done no other: teaching, I was coming to understand, is my native way of being in the world.'[3]

I feel I'm arriving rather late to the party of true vocation, yet this exploration over the last couple of years has led me to the understanding that much of what I was spending my time doing, whilst in part helpful, was not being true to myself and indeed at times was dangerous both to my own health and potentially toxic to those around me. It took me some time to realize that my body and my psyche and indeed through them my true self were trying to get my attention, wanting me to stop and discover my truth and authentic vocation. Through bouts of sickness, as well as being diagnosed with anxiety and depression, I eventually stopped running from the darkness that I thought would envelope me and turned to face it. I'm still learning to befriend it, however in that darkness lies a spark of light that has slowly led to an emerging sense of my vocation. A core part of it is writing. It's hard to explain the peace and contentment I often feel sitting at a keyboard and watching words appear on the screen. As Palmer found, there are clues in my past that point to writing and even academia, but they took some time to uncover. Oh and I do find myself a little agitated if I haven't written something in a while. There is a sense of, 'I couldn't not do this.'

Into this mix I'm discovering that my primary vocation is to be with God. As this emerged I struggled with it and immediately fell back into my 'production mentality' default. If being with God was to be my primary vocation then I thought I have to spend four, six, eight hours a day *with* him to be successful. Now, I never achieved that but the sentiment was real. Over time I began to see that whilst I needed to embrace a more contemplative spirituality I could actually cultivate a sense of being with God in the everyday. Through contemplative prayer, guidance from my spiritual director, sitting with Scripture and semi-regular retreats I am beginning to learn what it means to operate out of my true self being more

2. Palmer, *Let Your Life Speak*, 21.
3. Palmer, *Let Your Life Speak*, 21.

aware of God's constant presence. It is delightful to recognize him in nature, even in my inner city surrounds, but more to look for him in the other and on finding him seek to let the Christ in me meet the Christ in them.

Please don't get me wrong. This is a journey in progress and I feel like I am only taking baby steps, but I wanted to include this reflection here as a beacon or flag, perhaps a check-in as you approach the mission you feel called to. If you are to be authentic and real, and call those qualities out in others, then there needs to be a sense that what you are involved in and working towards is a reflection of who you have been created to be. Not who you think you should be, and not even a reflection of those that might inspire you, but truly you.

Related to this, I was recently reflecting on an experience I had whilst working for a Christian youth and community organization. I was having a meeting with the director, who I admired greatly, about my role. He named that he thought I would like something that reflected research and development. I brushed that off, because I perceived something like that would not be valued by the movement, which was very action orientated. Interestingly enough the director was onto something, but I let my ego and my desire to be seen as important in the movement get in the way of something that I now believe may have been truer to who I was created to be.

There isn't space for me to go into a lot of detail around contemplative spirituality and its links to mission and activism, but I'm learning the two aren't as separate as I originally thought they might be. In fact contemplation can fuel and ground activism in a way nothing else can. Whether its via following the daily office through morning and evening prayer, regular walks in nature, artistic practice, music, journaling, time in Scripture or a myriad of other practices, to live a sustainable missional life you need to slow down and spend time where your spirit can connect with God's spirit and you can experience his refreshing touch. Without that we become tired and brittle as does our work. We need time where the mind can slow down and become present with what is around us, where we can truly enjoy family and friends and experience the joy of connection with them. It's helpful to remember that self-care is not selfish. Without it we will eventually have nothing to offer anyone else and we just might find the true self protesting in rather loud and unseemly ways.

Another key aspect on the missional journey is a keen missional imagination that is rooted in the kind of deep spirituality that we have been exploring.

Re-capturing A Missional Imagination

There are many creative expressions of mission happening all over the globe. I was pleasantly surprised while talking with a former missionary to Malawi in Africa who told me about his work in communities where Islam was the majority religion. He and his family first went there over twenty years ago to plant churches. They realized early on in their work that the traditional approach was not going to cut it. Instead they invested in the social networks that were already present and engaged in projects that were going to serve the community, even working for a number of years in re-forestation. Through these projects they built relationships and began Bible studies, which over time grew in numbers. This is just one example of mission work that is true to God's broad agenda in the world as well as engaging in a real community need.

Basil of Caesarea

One of the early saints that engaged in this kind of thinking and action was Basil of Caesarea or Saint Basil the Great. He was born in 330CE to a wealthy family known for their religious convictions. His grandfather on his mother's side was a martyr, executed before Constantine made Christianity the state religion. Basil was formally educated in Cappadocia, in what is now Turkey. There he met Gregory of Nazianzus who would become his life-long friend. In later study he also met Julian the Apostate who would become emperor of Rome. Back in Caesarea he practiced law and taught ethics. An encounter with a charismatic bishop and ascetic would change his trajectory. He decided to leave his legal practice and devote his life to God.

In his zeal he travelled to Palestine, Egypt, Syria and Mesopotamia to study ascetics and monasticism. He also distributed his possessions to the poor and went into solitude near Neocaesarea of Pontus, again in modern day Turkey. As much as he admired the ascetics, he realized that the solitary life did not call him. There is also evidence that one of his turning points was a letter from his sister encouraging him to stop complaining about the state of the church, come back and make a difference.

So in 358 CE Basil returned to his family estate. Feeling drawn to communal life he gathered a group of like-minded disciples around him and founded a monastic settlement on the estate. He was joined by his widowed mother and sister, who devoted their lives to prayer and charitable works. Some even claim it was his sister who started the community. He established a rule of life incorporating a balance between prayer and work.

As well as creating a monastic movement Basil's concern for the poor never wavered. Legend has it that the estate was always open to the broader community and there was a steady flow of people in and out of the monastery to tend the gardens and receive the aid that they needed. Basil opened a soup kitchen as a result of a significant drought, feeding the poor and those without adequate supplies. As part of his work he was a staunch advocate for the poor and his other beliefs, such as the essential unity between the members of the Trinity. Through his letters we come to understand that he worked to reform thieves and prostitutes. Along these lines perhaps his most significant contribution was the building of the Basiliad just outside Caesarea. It housed accommodation, a hospice and a hospital.[4]

Basil is a great example of missional thinking and practice for a number of reasons. He built a community of like-minded people around him, who were committed to the connection between monastics and the rest of the community. This was quite radical as most monastics of the time lived in solitude, believing they needed to be separate to the world. Basil also sought to create a balance between prayer and work evidenced in his rule of life, so his missional output was rooted in a deep, informed spirituality. With effective community and a deeply rooted spirituality as the basis he was able to sustain a life that was given away to others. He also recognized that the thrust of the gospel wasn't only verbal, but led to action that would ultimately benefit the poor. With the building of the Basiliad, Basil cemented a relationship between church, or in his case, monastery and life changing mission.

Base Ecclesial Communities (BEC)

BEC is another example of creative effectual engagement with local communities. Sometimes in the West we believe we have the monopoly on

---

4. Joseph McSorley, "St. Basil the Great," in *The Catholic Encyclopedia*, (New York: Robert Appleton Company, 1907), accessed 9 March, 2016, http://www.newadvent.org/cathen/02330b.htm.

good ideas and innovation, but when it comes to small church and enabling the gifts of every person in a church, Latin America, the home of Liberation Theology, was ahead of most movements. Starting in the 1950s as part of the Catholic Church, the BEC are characterized by small groups, where people know each other and where individuality is expressed. They were a specific response to a hierarchical model of church with passive congregants.[5] The core question for the BEC was, how can the community experience of faith be embedded and structured in the conditions of a people who are both religious and oppressed?[6] Even though most of the original communities were started by a priest or someone from a religious order, the BEC are essentially a lay movement, with the laity involved in every level of decision making.

The BEC were initially started in response to an old lady who noticed the protestant Churches in her community celebrating Christmas, whilst for lack of a priest, the Catholic Church was silent. A local bishop then trained lay people to do everything that they could do within the bounds of current ecclesiastical discipline. Through this the internal life of the Catholic Church flourished, as people found gifts and the avenues to contribute. Pretty soon meeting halls, instead of chapels, were built and used for other endeavours such as education, sewing lessons and meetings to solve community problems.[7] Through this we see a group of people whose faith was interacting with everyday life.

Within the BEC there was an absence of alienating structures as well as the positive contribution that direct relationships can make. People were encouraged to interact with each other and reciprocity, deep communion, mutual assistance, gospel ideals and the equality of members saw the BEC become a living church. Central to their belief and practice was the building of the Kingdom of God, with individual and corporate liberation being a key theme.

Leonardo Boff, advocate for the BEC, believes they can be a useful counterpoint to the institutional church. Provided they don't see themselves as the only expression of community and church. Instead they can point to

---

5.   Petro Demo cited in Leonardo Boff, *Ecclesio-Genesis: The Base Communities Reinvent the Church* (London, UK: Collins, 1977), 1.

6.   Boff, *Ecclesio-Genesis*, 37.

7.   Boff, *Ecclesio-Genesis*, 3.

the need for evangelical authenticity and help the institution move closer to the ideal of community. This is a clear example of the margins talking to the centre, and beginning to have an impact. In my conversations with church leaders I often advocate for a similar approach, when there is a group of people within an established church that want to do things differently. My persuasion is to encourage them to move forward but to create opportunities for the stories to be told and the adventures shared with the broader church. Boff also makes the point that the alternate community needs to not see itself over and above the institutional church. Unfortunately within the emerging church scene in Australia, there has been a degree of arrogance towards the established church, and, I am sad to say, over time I have shared in this arrogance. However, an arrogance-born adversarial stance towards others in the body does not serve any cause well.

Within the Catholic Church of the mid twentieth century there were differing opinions around the validity of the BEC, some seeing that the BEC only had ecclesial elements that did not constitute a Church. However, the view prevailed that the Church existed in the people of God, encouraged by the Word and the discipleship of Christ.[8]

Leadership was still a crucial element within the BEC, for the facilitation of a grassroots, bottom-up community of faith. Through effective leadership the BEC fostered each person's particular gift and role within the community. This was recognized as part of the salvific event and a form of the manifestation of the Spirit within the community for its building up. I think sometimes in the Protestant Church we have missed the wholeness of what we are offered in Christ. The discovering of gift was seen as part of the journey of salvation. For us we can tend to separate the two with the latter becoming merely functional and perhaps not seen as spiritual.

The BEC were also concerned about the socio-political environment that they were a part of. In July 1978 there was a significant meeting within the Catholic Church in Latin America, where it began to realize the powerful effect of giving people voice and role. The poor of the BEC were allowed to speak, demonstrating that together they had begun to form a response to their poverty after being oppressed for 480 years. They stated that their oppression was due to the elitist, exclusive capitalist system. They articulated that liberation is achieved to the extent of their unification and creation of a

---

8.   Boff, *Ecclesio-Genesis*, 3.

network of grassroots movements.[9] By the next meeting in 1981 the power of participation and organization was even more obvious.

The BEC were able to integrate faith and life. They recognized the subversive nature of Jesus and the Word, using it as a source of life in their struggle against oppressive circumstances. They saw very clearly God's concern for, lordship over and presence in society. They recognized God as just and the one who stood with them in their struggles against oppression. They taught that one can't separate being Christian from crying out for justice. They built the Kingdom through the mediation of justice and love, a submission in solidarity as a communion of persons.[10]

As the BEC communities were created, associations of every kind were also created. The overarching aim of these associations was to refashion the social fabric and rebuild the people as agents of their own fate, set with the task of building a livable community for all. 'And politics is the mighty weapon we have, to build a just society the way God wants it.'[11] This struggle for a just society is not based on a causal enthusiasm, rather a strong sense of the arduous nature of their journey and the reality of communitas that this creates. We of course experience our relationship with Christ and the Word through the lens of where we sit, but Boff's point of the struggle for a just society not being based on casual enthusiasm is a good one, particularly in our age of 'clicktivism' where there is temptation to believe that we have done our bit through clicking 'like' or signing an online survey, enabling us to go onto the next cause. Again, this is where contemplation is such an important part of activism. We will not be able to respond to the number of causes that come to our attention, but through contemplation the invitation is to go deep inside ourselves, to meet with God there and listen to the promptings that our inner being is making. Then we can respond from that point of meeting with ourselves and with God. This process leads to a deeper, more sustained response, perhaps to a single issue based on God's heart for the poor.

As they relate to missional imagination, the BEC teach us again the importance of community and the power present as a group of people work towards a picture of the Kingdom of God in their context. Added to this,

---

9.   Boff, *Ecclesio-Genesis*, 35.

10. Boff, *Ecclesio-Genesis*, 41.

11. Boff, *Ecclesio-Genesis*, 43.

through the BEC our imagination is heightened to the cause of justice, not only for individuals but collectively as a people.

Basil and the BEC are two examples of mission that seek to hold in tension the draw towards God's Kingdom including his desire for justice, and as part of this the need for community to be a sustaining practice and an engine room for change. Both Basil and the BEC had the whole community in view as they sought to do mission. So often in our context mission has been about the saving of individual souls. I see people moving towards God more as a consequence of seeking first the Kingdom in a community. As we do this a good place to start is research.

Research: A Place to Start

My first research project was a needs based analysis centred on a geographical region around a church in the northern suburbs of Adelaide. I'm not sure what the research achieved for the community. It did help us understand our neighbourhood, which was different to where the church was originally set up. Unfortunately, due to internal issues, the church largely continued as it had, which led to a disconnect with its adopted community. As alluded in the asset mapping phase of ABCD, context is everything. Groups from churches to social services, local council, state and federal governments, sporting clubs and so on have made the same mistake of viewing the community through the lens of what they want to offer, or even the identity of their organization. In Pakenham, it was quite common for new services or programs to arrive on the doorstep, as it were, with very little or no consultation with the community or the existing services, inevitably causing some ruffling of the feathers amongst the other workers. This was not such an issue in itself. Of more concern was the effect these new services would have on the community. Don't get me wrong, the services weren't bad in themselves, but due to not doing research they were unaware of the aspirations of the community and how the service might benefit or otherwise those aspirations. They were also unaware of the nuances of the community and how best to communicate what they had to offer.

This highlights a related issue - the focus of the majority of social services, and to some extent churches tends to be on the individual. We tend to look at community work from a medical model, which seeks to address the need of the person in front of us, seeing them as a unit outside of their family or community networks. The emphasis is slowly shifting to recognize the importance of the community around someone for their recovery or progression towards flourishing, however we have a long way to go. This is particularly true for the type of programs that receive funding from all levels of government. Because it is easier to quantify, services that focus on individual or at best family wellness will get funded over ideas that seek to build community. Family and even extended family use to be the basic building block of society, but with the high incidence of family breakdown, in many instances, I suspect, we will need to create supports within the broader community that allows for the healing of individuals and families.

As well as rebuilding community around people, one of the key ways to help is to re-infuse a sense of purpose into their lives, which can be a result of building your asset map. Earlier I showed that as you begin to unearth people's gold or hidden skills, they can become quite excited about discovering opportunities to contribute those skills to the broader picture.

Understanding the people that make up your community is an essential part of effective community development. What are their aspirations? What skills do they have towards those aspirations? Do they know others who share their interests? This way you become an activator within your community. In this way research is not only for new services or churches. I can almost guarantee that as you embark on an exploration of this nature you will discover things you were unaware of or, at the very least, new perspectives to take into your community work.

Whilst you may not adopt ABCD or the Appreciative Inquiry approach outlined in the first chapter in their entirety, they embody the attitude that is necessary for successful community work. They see the glass as half full, recognizing the good that is inherent in communities and seek avenues to draw out those positives. Again this doesn't mean that you become glibly unaware of the issues. The strengths, the positives, simply become the starting point.

A strength based approach also prevents us coming to our communities with a saviour mentality. This can be a subtle intrusion into truly loving and valuing the local community and relates to the view we hold as to why people are poor or in need. As saviours we inevitably believe that people are poor because of their own doing and are in need of rescuing. This fails to take into account the effects of long-term poverty, poor education, being misunderstood, a system that values production and tends to ignore, or worse, discriminate against people who are different or who are perceived to not belong. The idea that we need to rescue these people means that we believe we hold the key to undoing their poverty and if they would only listen to us then they would be okay. Believing that we need to rescue others subtly puts us above them and prevents us from true empathy or mercy. This doesn't mean we don't have anything to offer. It means that our first role as people seeking to engage and benefit a community is to value those we are working with. To sit long enough to hear their stories, to be moved by their courage and tenacity as survivors and to help them realize the skills and potentials they have. And to honour the cry of 'nothing for us without us.' [12] This means that we invite them to the shared planning table and that the ones whom we are connecting with become the leaders and the ones who can then journey with others. It may feel a bit upside down, yet how like God to want to use the ones who are seen as foolish in the eyes of the world. Our role also changes from upfront leaders to servants, again resonating with Jesus' words and actions.

Organizing ourselves in such a way takes a gritty commitment to the ones we are seeking to serve. The challenge is to recognize each person as created and loved, not an object to change or a project to complete. In fact they are people who can bring us joy, whom we can learn from and in this way we build mutuality with them. In turn each community has the potential to reflect the Kingdom of God. In the ruggedness of life there can be the opportunity for people from all walks of life to connect and discover a sense of belonging, a safety net in which to explore their world. Research is key to unpacking these potentials in individuals and communities.

I am lucky enough to know many wonderful people who believe in the potential of others in this way and are working on a picture of the Kingdom in their communities. Let me share just a few of their stories with you.

---

12. The sentiment has a long history in various movements. I first came across it in relation to the South African disability rights movement and it is attributed to Michael Masutha and William Rowland.

Stories from the Field

Derek Bradshaw and the Now and Not Yet Community

I went out to Warrandyte (a leafy suburb in the North East of Melbourne) to meet with Derek in the café that the faith community run. It's set on the main street of the town with a rustic interior and décor, very appropriate for the alternative community that they serve. The café serves great coffee and food seven days a week, catering for a population that actively look out for each other and connect, cultivating a sense of belonging over coffee. The community is such that no chain outlets like McDonald's or 7Eleven have been allowed to set up. As well as people seeking an alternate lifestyle, the community is known for its arts and music, and people who seek spirituality in a whole range of ways, searching for their place in the world.

Derek, an ordained minister, was approached by his denomination to consider church planting. He initially wasn't keen about the idea but as he was praying about it in the Warrandyte community God gave him a vision of what could be and the faith community have worked on achieving that vision. The café itself doesn't have much to badge it as a Christian affair, there is no 'Jesus saves' message or giant cross on the wall. Derek sees that many of the symbols and catchphrases that we might use to designate church are dripping with negative connotations for the non-religious. However the Now and Not Yet community are living the essence of church.

They have set a tone of relational engagement in the style of the broader community and they seek to live the values of the Kingdom of God in the way they interact, their relationship with staff and volunteers and even their response to difficult customers or people looking for a meal who might not be able to pay. What they are doing is not framed as a church, but they live and breathe the essence of a community of God's people. They seek to remove the barriers to faith that church often creates. Because of their relational approach and their obvious care for people, they are quite often asked why they are doing what they are doing and this provides the opportunity for Derek and other members of the faith community to simply share their lives - not preach, but talk about their motivations.

In addition, Derek and his crew take a positive or strength based approach to the Warrandyte community. It's not a lower socio-economic community with obvious systemic needs. It even has a Facebook page that members of the community can access and share individual need. Once this is done people very quickly respond. The strength of the community is evidenced when there are crises such as a fire at the pub. Once news of the fire spread, the pub was inundated with patronage - yes people wanting to hear what happened, but more, wanting to help the pub get back on its feet.

Derek believes that rather than setting up to run programs, a better approach in a community like Warrandyte is to get on board with what is already happening, and so supporting businesses like the pub is very important. They have even gone as far as forming a partnership with the pub and the local Bendigo Bank to create a community garden which will eventually generate micro enterprises for interested members of the community. In addition they offer opportunity for members of the community to volunteer in the café, in this way helping them to become work ready. And fitting in with the arts and music scene they offer guitar making courses onsite in a section of the café.

The philosophy behind the way the Now and Not Yet community engages with Warrandyte is simple. God is present everywhere, the challenge becomes whether or not as people of faith we'll be postured towards it. Derek sees that everyone is made in the image of God, even the person who is drunk at the pub. They are no less in God's image than he is and so the valuing of people and the way we interact with them becomes crucial messaging about who God is and what is important to him.[13]

Dr David Wilson, CEO Urban Seed

David's journey with faith and community development, dates back to the 1970s and his involvement with the Jesus Movement. He started a community called God's House Street Church. Although at the time they didn't recognize it as community development, they were incarnational, seeking to walk alongside people who were suffering from drug addiction and mental health issues. They sought out the strengths of these people, connecting with them through their drop-in centre. The centre was an old converted church from which they had removed all the pews, replacing them with couches, bean bags, table tennis and a pool table. The centre was open six days a week and three nights. They also had five community houses associated with the work, where many of the people they connected with

---

13. You can find out more about the Now and Not Yet Café at https://www.facebook.com/nowandnotyetcafe/.

who were homeless found refuge. The core element that the community offered those they connected with was belonging.

For David there has always been an inherent link between his faith and community development. He understands that by following Jesus we must seek to do what he did, which was work to develop his community. Without this connection our faith doesn't make sense. David understands that there is a difference between community development outcomes and methods. He believes you can achieve CD outcomes through interventionist and welfare approaches. However, these aren't anywhere near as effective or empowering as working from a CD methodology that recognizes the journey as equally important if not more important than the outcome. The methodology acknowledges that everyone has assets to bring to the table and gives them the opportunity to bring them.

David's current role is CEO of Urban Seed, a community development organization with headquarters right in the heart of Melbourne's CBD. They work with some of the most marginalized and vulnerable people who inhabit the local streets and laneways. Through meals, art groups and other ventures they seek to create a sense of belonging that enables significant relationships to be formed, and skills to be unearthed. One of their slow burn projects is the development of a social enterprise that will provide employment for some and work readiness training for others.

This project and others within Urban Seed would not be possible without recognizing and valuing the importance of partnerships with other organizations that can help share the costs and receive the benefits. In talking about partnerships with David we uncovered an issue that some churches and other organizations face - the fear of association. Essentially this is about being painted with the same brush that the other organization might be. So, for example, the Now and Not Yet Community is partnering with a pub. Some outside of that partnership may not be comfortable with either side of the equation, so potentially there could be a fear on either side. A way to overcome this is to acknowledge upfront that there are things both hold in common and other things that they would not. However, there is enough common ground to work together for the common good of the community. This can then be explained to any detractor. A partnership based on a CD project is a good way to demonstrate this.

Partnerships lead naturally to seeing the Kingdom of God alive and active in a community. David lived in the CBD for eleven years and during that time was continually aware of the good done by a diverse range of organizations and that in fact these organizations were bringing about the Kingdom even if they didn't use that language to describe what they were doing. David saw that any approximation towards the Kingdom, i.e. the creation of justice or any aspect of shalom was worth celebrating. To David this is the essence of CD and in fact is akin to Kingdom development.[14]

Neal Taylor, CEO Holy Fools and Chaplain to the Homeless in the Yarra Ranges

Around ten years ago Neal and his family made the decision to begin serving the homeless in their community. Initially this involved Neal joining existing community meals, run by some of the churches in his local area. These meals would feed a couple of hundred people a week. However, Neal became frustrated with their approach which, whilst being very loving and offering a listening ear to people's issues, did not foster relationships with them outside of the meals. So Neal started doing some chaplaincy work in the community. This involved spending more time with individuals, getting to know them and talking through their issues in more depth, working to help them create a plan to move forward. As necessary he would also attend police interviews, hospital and accompany people to court.

Holy Fools itself started in 2009, initially as a structure for Neal to do his work and create legitimacy around it. His hope was to broaden the focus of the meals happening within Croydon, but God had other plans. Neal's focus shifted to Lilydale and the Yarra Ranges. Whilst Croydon has a bit of a reputation for homelessness and marginalization, the leafy Lilydale did not and so it came as a surprise to many people that there was even an issue of homelessness and entrenched poverty in the community. One of Neal's core responses has been to raise awareness of and advocate for the plight of the homeless in Lilydale, highlighting that the issue is as much a concern in the outer suburbs as in the CBD. And in fact people experiencing poverty in the outer suburbs are often at more of a disadvantage because government policy tends to not cater for those issues in suburbs that, at least on the surface, appear more affluent.

---

14. To find out more information about Urban Seed visit, http://www.urbanseed.org.

Neal comments that we tend to hold a stereotypical view of homelessness - the middle aged man, with a matted beard and an odour, carrying a bottle, who is sleeping rough. In fact he is seeing a new face to homelessness in Melbourne and around Australia, with many families becoming the new working poor. The slippery slope to homelessness and the need to sleep in a car or the garage of a kind friend can be very fast. Neal reports to knowing families that within a week after losing a job or some other crisis find themselves losing their home and their situation becoming a whole lot more desperate.

As a response Neal, with the Holy Fools team, has sought to raise awareness of the plight of those struggling in the Yarra Ranges as well as seek to alleviate some immediate need. He discovered that in the Yarra Ranges community there were only a couple of other overwhelmed agencies working in a similar way. Filling a gap, Holy Fools has provided much needed resources for families and struggling individuals, including toiletries, swags, blankets and food. Systemically people are discovering that there is no easy fix to being homeless, with a shortage of accommodation across the valley. This can leave people despondent and angry, leading to some turning to drugs and others suffering mental health issues, which of course can lead to further entrenchment in poverty.

Into this negative cycle Holy Fools seeks to input presence, love, compassion and ultimately hope. They provide a listening ear and a heart that says you are our brother or sister, let us help you, and even carry you for a while. Sounding like a welfare approach, inherent in these objectives is a community development methodology that recognizes there is a time in people's lives when they need extra support. However, it is ultimately not helpful to leave them in that place. So as trust is built Neal is able to speak positively into people's lives, drawing out from them their strengths and reminding them of their resilience. A tougher task is building community amongst this group of people. However, through work like Street Angels, a weekly lunch running in two locations, Neal and a small team of volunteers seek to build a web of support that is empowering. They regularly remind people that this is only a transition phase and that within themselves they have incredible capacity to turn things around.

This journey can be slow. Neal journeyed with Mick over a twelve-month period. Mick started by helping the team pack up after the lunchtime Street

Angels. Overtime he began to relax with Neal, sharing some of his struggles. He eventually got to a place of trust where he asked for counselling to continue the journey of restoration. This came about through the renewed relational web that was built by the community around him.

Neal and others working with the marginalized in our communities quite often state their motivation as following what they see Jesus doing. This is a simple way of recognizing that the originator of any community work done in his name is Jesus. He was willing to presence himself (incarnate) with us, and whilst he could have been King, he chose to serve with love and compassion. He is our guide when it comes to community engagement. Through the gospel story Neal sees Jesus spending time with people who are on the margins, caring, engaging in conversation, consulting with them about what they wanted and beginning in them the journey of transformation.[15]

Like others who have gone before him, Neal is only too aware of his own shortcomings and sin and uses this awareness to convey God's unconditional love to many that society deem unlovable.

Lee Palumbo – Co-Founder Just Planet and Manager Sunbury Community House

Lee and her husband Norman moved to Sunbury after they finished theological college in 2006. As a person of faith, Lee sees a direct connection between her faith and community development. As a social enterprise café and fair trade supplier, their shop Just Planet is a tool to bring a diverse community together and help get projects off the ground in a more unified way. Whilst being aware of some of the challenges of Sunbury and its reputation, Lee and Norman chose to see the positives in the community. One thing that struck Lee early on was the generosity of the butcher next door to the shop, giving sausages to the Rotary BBQ that was set up late on a Friday night to feed those coming out of the nightclub. It was subtle examples like this that began to show the community's strength and potential.

Just Planet was a response to the couple's time at theological college. They graduated with an understanding that the gospel pointed to the need to act in the community, and that the community gathered around shops and

---

15. To find out more information about Holy Fools visit www.holyfools.org.au.

cafés. Just Planet started as a fair trade store and developed into a café with shared tables. Lee and Norman's aim was to engage with existing things in the community and by being on the main street they are in an ideal place to communicate those things.

By engaging with what the community was already doing they resisted the temptation to get involved in welfare. Instead of setting up special services for those in need they established a pay-it-forward system at the café. This allowed them to become sensitive and respond to the needs of those who were experiencing hard times. Both Lee and Norman recognize that everyone goes through hard times, including themselves, and by establishing such a system they maintained a friendly, non-threatening way to offer help. Plus it gave the opportunity for the community to support each other.

Lee believes that at times people in the Church portray an image that says everything is ok, that somehow help can only be offered if it comes from a place of strength. This fails to recognize we are all part of a broken humanity, and are all in the same boat. Through the shared table at Just Planet, Lee and Norman have witnessed people from all backgrounds connect together and form the most amazing relationships, many a conversation being prompted by the words they leave on the table.

As well as individual connections, Lee and Norman have fostered partnerships within the Sunbury community. Their approach has been to watch and observe, joining with some of the projects already happening in the town. For example, the local council had extensive gardening works, so instead of starting their own, they got on board and promoted the good work already being done. Lee believes that partnerships are the only way for the future, they combat organizational ego and lend mutual credibility. Just Planet is approached by all kinds of groups for informal partnership. A recent example was the local hairdresser who was promoting her 'Shave For A Cure' event. Lee sees that partnerships in themselves model good community development, showing that we can do more together than on our own. The other benefit is rubbing shoulders with people of like heart or mind, who might not share the faith but have a similar vision for the outcome of a project. There is a lovely co-operative action that grows, each event building on the other.

Faith and community development are integrally linked in Lee's thinking. Some Christians see that the gospel is only shared once the story of Jesus is told. Lee and Norman took a different approach. When the couple started work in Sunbury, Norman was a licensed minister and because of the way they worked in the community, relationships formed. When the big events or struggles happened in life, quite often people would come to them. In those moments they were surprised to discover that Norman was a minister, but happy to have him involved in their lives in that capacity.

The couple have a strong belief in authenticity and have shared their own struggles as a family with friends in the community. Lee understands that you don't have to be perfect to live the gospel and in fact it is better demonstrated in the brokenness, pain and struggle of life. Since coming to faith she has seen the reality of the world and recognizes Jesus as the one who calls us to stand in authenticity with those who are suffering. As they were finishing college they were looking for the revolution that would bring transformation to society. Unfortunately they did not find it in the churches. They realized that God was present in the community and that they could be the Church out there.

Because of this focus Lee and Norman were looking for the goodness already present in the community. They believe it is those assets that are the transforming power for the future. For Sunbury these include a community that is very family focused, keen on sports and enjoys gatherings more of the family fun-day and sausage sizzle type than the art exhibition. The starting point for Lee and Norman was informal research where they looked, listened, observed and reflected on the community and its interests, with the resolve to be present in those interests. They lament the lack of involvement of the traditional church in this type of approach, believing there is so much potential for its involvement. Churches can struggle to be involved because they believe outside agencies have other agendas. Alternatively, Lee sees that we are all talking about the social fabric, so there is plenty of room to work together. Her encouragement is for churches to look at the small things that are happening in a community - the one-on-one conversations, the connections made, the small scale projects embarked upon - and watch those spread and permeate through the community to change and transform it.

Lee takes the idea of transformation into her role at the Sunbury Community House, seeing that faith informs everything that she does in her community development practice. Each activity or course that the house runs is in response to a need or aspiration of the community, which is discovered through consultation. The aim is then to make that activity or course as accessible as possible, even to the extent of people who have employment subsidizing those who don't. Lee believes that a tokenistic response from government to the issues in a community doesn't cut it and in fact there needs to be a groundswell up, informing policy makers and funders what is right and just for the local community.[16]

A Debate We Need to Have

Lee's thought on the need for a groundswell up approach to policy, as opposed to a top down engagement, is a helpful bridge to the final section of this book. Government tends to fund a welfare approach to service delivery, quite often regardless of the feelings of the recipient community. I realized again how entrenched this approach is when recently talking with the CEO of a large community housing organization. I was sharing with him about a strength-based approach to development. I could see that he was interested, stepping back, taking time to reflect, coming back to me with an informed response, applying the thinking internally to aspects of the organization. I can't recall exactly how the conversation changed, but despite acknowledging that individuals need community and that we are healthier this way, we came to his reality that the government would never fund a community development approach to housing and that is kind of where the conversation ended, much to my disappointment.

Many churches have also become entrenched in the welfare model of service delivery, but perhaps for different reasons. On a first reading of the gospels and parts of the Old Testament there seems to be an emphasis on the alleviation of poverty. This has often been translated into our own version of a top down approach. The church is here and we will provide you with what you need, which could include a meal, a place to stay for the night, warm clothes or blankets; we may even give you a food voucher as you go on your way. I believe all of this is motivated by compassion, a sense of justice or any number of other good motivations. However, I also

---

16. For more information on Just Planet go to https://www.facebook.com/Just-Planet-Fair-Trade-Gift-Shop-Cafe-123770597719490/ or http://www.justplanet.net/.

believe we have a problem when we see the same people coming to the same services over a five, ten or even fifteen year period with very little change in their circumstances. A core question for us that comes from this - is it enough for us to provide some temporary help and leave people in their poverty? Are we in fact helping?

Jesus said that the poor will always be with you, but this wasn't a justification for leaving people exactly where they are. Many of the miracles that Jesus performed such as healing, freeing from demonic possession and so on actually enabled people to participate in society once again. So how can our helping enable people to participate in society towards a thriving and flourishing life? I recently completed a large piece of work for a faith based housing organization. The aim of the project was to uncover what was unique about the way the organization operated. One key factor emerged around hospitality. When there is true love and acceptance for someone as they are, a profound sense of welcome is established. The organization stated that they don't expect people to change. In fact they respect them too much for that. However, through the environment created within their large houses, people do begin to change. For the first time in perhaps years or ever, many residents find themselves progressing from a survival mode to a space where they can reflect on life, discover more about who they are, the strengths they have and often they begin to try new things.

Whilst every church or organization is not able to offer accommodation in this way, I think the faith based housing organization may hold an important key to the approach we need to take as people of faith. We can't put as one of our KPIs the number of people who have realized their internal strengths and abilities and are now productive citizens as a result of our program. If we do that, we create a rod for our backs and for those we are attempting to help. However, in the unconditional welcome that hospitable relationships provide there is space that allows the external masks to be dropped and self to be explored in a potentially transformative way. I believe this is what leads to effective community development that enables people to participate and contribute to the places they find themselves. This is a counter measure to the predominant welfare model that many are beginning to question for a whole range of reasons.

However, I fear the CEO I mentioned at the top of this section is right. Government will not fund the sorts of initiatives that will begin to change the game for so many. Part of the reason for this is their preoccupation with evidenced based outcomes and short-term results, which inevitably leave people stuck. The alternative is for churches, community groups, passionate individuals and those services flexible enough to work on different agendas coming together. First, to dream dreams with those on the margins, of how the world could be. Then to work together with those on the margins to see the dawning of those dreams and what could eventually be the beginning of a new day. What we're talking about is the creation with God of communities that reflect the Kingdom.

Reflection Questions

1. For those of us who share the faith, our spirituality or relationship with God is key. How are you going at maintaining that relationship?

2. Parker Palmer talks about letting your life speak. This is referring to the authentic you. Without this authenticity our mission can become toxic to those we are trying to help. As you think about these things, what is really driving you to be involved in the work you are doing?

3. What inspires you about Basil of Caesarea, the base ecclesial communities or one of the stories from the field?

4. Where do you sit in the welfare vs empowerment debate? Why?

Conclusion

My aim in writing this book is to help people of faith embrace community development, and grow to see, appreciate and partner with others working in the space. I long for God's people to see community development as a valid form of mission and one that reflects God's heart to see communities of the Kingdom established wherever we find ourselves.

Our journey started with a snapshot into the Australian community, focusing on young people as a litmus test or canary in the mine, by which to view how Australia is going at caring for the vulnerable among us. As part of this exploration we acknowledged that within any community there are both murky and marvellous elements. Community development tools such as Appreciative Inquire (AI) and Asset Based Community Development (ABCD) teach us to focus on the positive, not disregarding the negative, but instead focusing on the strengths of individuals and communities as building blocks for internal transformation.

Individual and community transformation is a reflection of the created order. Scripture gives us a picture of the way the world could be (and will eventually be) and the role of the members of the Godhead or Trinity in both the creation and sustaining of the world. We see the Father as creator and understand that he enabled humankind to be stewards of his created order. We understand Jesus as liberator both for us personally but also for the world. Jesus' brand of liberation is not only spiritual but actually encompasses every aspect of our lives. This is demonstrated by Jesus' Sermon on the Mount where he outlines the characteristics of the blessed life, or the 'good life.' Through this section I sought to draw parallels between the Christian experience and similar expressions for those that don't own faith. This correlation is possible because wherever we witness the values of the Kingdom, it is present. Finally the role of the Holy Spirit is to apply the work of Jesus to us as individuals and provide the impetus and resources for transformation. The Holy Spirit is the source of anything good in the world. The effect of his or her presence is seen in Galatians 5 and evidenced in characteristics that we can live out in our lives.

As we begin to grasp just the edge of the roles of the individual members of the Trinity we realize that the Christian faith is incredibly earthy and related to this world. We are then left in a good space to explore different models of the Kingdom. Using Howard Snyder's continuum of eight models from a kingdom that is internalized and future focused to purely an earthly utopia, we recognize the breadth of interpretation of the Kingdom's activity in the world. Snyder hastens to point out that the models are constructs and no one model possesses the whole truth. We are encouraged to explore them and hold closest to the ones that don't seek to resolve the tensions that arise in the biblical witness.

In Chapter 4 we unpacked the Church's response to a Kingdom that is both present now but will be fully revealed in the future. It is an internal reality as well as a community manifestation. Despite what it might seem at times the Church was always meant to be inclusive. The idea of God choosing some and not others was really about some being chosen to be a blessing to others. Israel was a nation with a mission to show how a people could live under God. Likewise the Church is a people called out with the purpose of calling others to participate in God's dream for the world. Internally the core of the universal Church is the Eucharist. It binds us together in an act of remembrance and recommitment, connecting us to other saints both past and present.

As Chapter 4 continued it unpacked the development of the Church through Christendom which saw the coming together of church and state. Although we are in a post-Christendom era, it has still had a profound effect on the modern church. Through Constantine and then into the Middle Ages, the Church enjoyed a favoured position in society. Even today in our tax system there are still some advantages that ministers enjoy. This favour has left the Church with a sense of entitlement, despite its waning popularity amongst mainstream society, often meaning that the voice of the Church, whilst internally feeling strong, has come across like a squeaky high pitched whine. Please don't misunderstand me, the Church has a lot to offer into the current debates about the journey towards a better world. However, it has largely been locked out of these conversations due to a failure to effectively contextualize and understand a rapidly shifting world and its changing status within that world. Even while this might seem bleak, within our culture there are many stamps of the divine, waiting for the people of God to recognize them and incorporate them into God's mission in the world.

To see and incorporate these signs, the people of God in a local community need to own their connectedness to the broader body of Christ as well as beginning to seriously explore their neighbourhood. Their theology of building and space becomes a key aspect of missional engagement. Other internal attitudes include a commitment to prayer and Scripture. As the people of God we need to be authentic, which includes being real about our struggles and doubts. Related to this, the hallmark of the gathered and dispersed community is to be love. The quality of our love for each other is what will draw people towards God, as well as modelling the way the world could be. Love leads us naturally to hospitality, offering an unconditional welcome to all. Lastly we need to recognize our transitional state in the world and invest in each other and our shared mission in such a way that deep community or communitas is created.

After chapter 4, we began to move more towards the more practical end of the book. It is important for us to understand our broader cultural context and the journey toward it. Over the last five hundred years humanity has moved from being enchanted and porous, being acted upon by the forces of the world, to a more rational view that allows distance from and examination of events. Christianity played its part in this transition and with it the rise of exclusive humanism. More doctrines entered the faith which had previously been based on simple beliefs and actions. As well, belief became internalized and lost its legitimizing function in society. With the rise of science and rationalism there was an optimism that anything could be achieved in the advancement of the human race. However, after two world wars, an economic depression and many other negative events, disillusionment had begun to creep into society.

Response to this disillusionment began in the arts with a movement known as postmodernism. Amongst other things it questioned the nature of truth and the relevancy of an over-arching narrative. The movement recognizes our world as a place of hyperreality where the symbol of a product is worth as much if not more than the product itself. Essentially postmodernism demonstrates to us the complexity of the world we live in and the need for the Church to re-examine its cultural maps.

Liberation theology then gives us some insight into how to do this and links with the practical community development tool, ABCD. Within liberation theology there are three mediations that point towards an orthopraxis or right action: social (understanding the context), hermeneutical (through the lens of Scripture), and practical (what action will be taken). If we use this theology as a basis we can clearly see that the five steps of ABCD point us towards a God-inspired connection with our community. Put simply, these five steps are: create an asset map, build relationships, encourage the creation of micro enterprises and buying local and understand the communication flows, draw the community together for visioning and planning, and as necessary partner with outside resources.

In the final chapter I move from the community to explore a more personal aspect of mission. It is essential that we work to develop a personal spirituality that will enliven and empower us to continue a genuine and life-giving engagement with our community, in whatever capacity we find ourselves. This spirituality will then become the engine room for our missional imagination and creativity. It will allow us to look at the world differently, through God's eyes, and respond from that place like Basil of Caesarea, those involved in Base Ecclesial Communities and others closer to home. Experiencing our community through God's eyes allows us to take the time to really see our communities and discover what life is like for them. The best way to do this is to start any community project with research. Get to know the geography, demography, the businesses, services, schools, churches and of course the people who live there. Explore their strengths and aspirations, work with them to continue the journey of community transformation.

Finally, I opened up a debate which we need to further wherever we can. The default in government, church and other service approaches is welfare. This ultimately sets the helper up to be the hero in the story and disempowers the ones we are seeking to help. The better approach is strength based community development, fuelled by an unconditional hospitality that doesn't expect change, but creates the opportunity and environment for it.

So as you continue to explore community engagement from a Christian perspective or are sympathetic to working with people of faith, may the originator and re-generator of communities, the image bearer, fill you with dreams, hopes and aspirations that reflect the divine and yet are available for all to participate in. God Bless.

Bibliography

Andrews, David. *Compassionate Community Work.* Carlisle: Piquant Editions, 2006.

Bayer, Charles, H. *A Guide to Liberation Theology for Middle-Class Congregations.* St Louis, MO: CBP Press, 1986.

Bonhoeffer, Dietrich. *Cost of Discipleship.* New York, NY: Touchstone, 1959.

Bonhoeffer, Dietrich. *Life together.* London: SCM, 1954.

Boff, Leonardo. *Church Charism and Power - Liberation Theology and the Institutional Church.* Chestnut Ridge, NY: Crossroad, 1985.

Boff, Leonardo. *Ecclesio-Genesis: The Base Communities Reinvent the Church.* London, UK: Collins, 1977.

Boff, Leonardo and Clovodis Boff. *Introducing Liberation Theology.* Kent: Burns & Oats, 1987.

Bosch, David J. *Transforming Mission: Paradigm Shifts in Theology of Mission.* Maryknoll, NY: Orbis, 1991.

Bright, John. *The Kingdom of God.* Nashville: Abingdon Press, 1990.

Cairns, Earl, E. *Christianity Through The Centuries.* Grand Rapids, MI: Zondervan, 1978.

Cram, Fiona. "Appreciative Inquiry." *MAI Review* 3, (2010): 1-13.

Fitch, David E. *Reclaiming the Mission of the Church from Big Business, Parachurch Organizations, Psychotherapy, Consumer Capitalism and Other Modern Maladies.* Grand Rapids, MI: Baker Books, 2005.

Frost, Michael. *Exiles: Living Missionally in a Post-Christian Culture.* Peabody, MA: Hendrickson, 2006.

Frost, Michael and Alan Hirsch. *The Shaping of Things to Come: Innovation and Mission for the 21st Century Church.* Erina, NSW: Strand, 2004.

Greene, Colin and Martin Robinson. *Metavista: Bible, Church and Mission in an age of Imagination.* Milton Keynes, UK: Authentic Media, 2008.

Guder, Darrell, ed. *Missional Church: A Vision for the Sending of the Church in North America*. Grand Rapids, MI: Eerdmans, 1989.

Gutenson, Charles E. *Christians and the Common Good: How Faith Intersects with Public Life*. Grand Rapids, MI: Brazos, 2011.

Gutierrez, Gustavo. *A Theology of Liberation*. Maryknoll, NY: Orbis, 1988.

Hartwich, Oliver. *A Global Perspective on Localism*. Hamilton, NZ: The New Zealand Initative and LGNZ, 2013.

Hirsch, Alan. *The Forgotten Ways: Reactivating the Missional Church*. Grand Rapids, MI: Brazos, 2006.

Hirst, John. *Looking for Australia*. Melbourne: Black Inc, 2010.

Ife, Jim. *Community Development: Creating community alternatives - vision, analysis and practice*. Melbourne, VIC: Longman, 1995.

Jones, E. Stanley. *Is The Kingdom of God Realism?* New York, NY: Abingdon, 1940.

Kretzman, John P. and John L. Mcknight. *Building Communities from the Inside Out: A Path Toward Finding and Mobilizing a Community's Assets*. Chicago, IL: ACTA, 1993.

Mangalwadi, Vishal. *The Book That Made Your World*. Grand Rapids, MI: Thomas Nelson, 2011.

McSorley, Joseph. "St. Basil the Great." In *The Catholic Encyclopedia*. New York: Robert Appleton Company, 1907. Accessed 9 March, 2016. http://www.newadvent.org/cathen/02330b.htm.

Miner, Maureen, Dowson, Miner & Devenish, Stuart. *Beyond Wellbeing: Spirituality and Human Flourishing*. USA: Information Age Publishing, 2012.

Moltmann, Jurgen. *In the End - The Beginning, the Life of Hope*. Minneapolis, MN: Fortress Press, 2004.

Moltmann, Jurgen. *The Trinity and the Kingdom of God: The Doctrine of God*. London: SCM, 1981.

Newbigin, Lesslie. *The Gospel in a Pluralist Society*. Grand Rapids, MI: Eerdmans, 1989.

Newbigin, Lesslie. *The Open Secret: An Introduction to the Theology of Mission.* Grand Rapids, MI: Eerdmans, 1995.

Newman, Martyn. *Liberation Theology is Evangelical.* Melbourne: Mallorn Press, 1990.

Nouwen, Henri J.M. *Reaching Out: Three Movements of the Spiritual Life.* New York, NY: Doubleday, 1975.

Novak, Michael. *Will It Liberate: Questions About Liberation Theology.* New York, NY: Paulist, 1986.

Palmer, Parker J. *Let Your Life Speak: Listening for the voice of vocation.* CA: John Wiley & Sons, 2000.

Pannenberg, Wolfhart. *Systematic Theology: Volume 3.* Grand Rapids, MI: 1997.

Robertson, E.H. *Dietrich Bonhoeffer.* London: Carey Kingsgate, 1966.

Roxburgh, Alan. *The Missionary Congregation, Leadership and Liminality.* Harrisburg, PA: Trinity Press, 1997.

Shelley, Bruce L. *Church History in Plain Language.* Dallas, TX: Word, 1995.

Sider, Ronald J., Philip Olso, and Heidi Unruh. *Churches That Make A Difference: Reaching your community with Good News and Good Works.* Grand Rapids, MI: Baker Books, 2002.

Snyder, Howard A. *Models of the Kingdom.* Nashville, TN: Abingdon Press, 1991.

Sobrino, Jon and Ignacio Ellacuria, eds. *Systematic Theology, Perspectives from Liberation Theology.* Maryknoll, NY: Orbis, 1996.

Stephenson, Carl and Bryce Lyon, eds. *Mediaeval History: Europe from the Second to Sixteenth Century.* New York, NY: Harper and Row, 1951.

Taylor, Charles. *A Secular Age.* Cambridge: Belknap of Harvard University, 2007.

Wright, N. Tom. *Surprised by Hope.* London: SPCK, 2007.

Online Articles

Burgess, Samuel. "Toowoomba: Queensland floods one year on." *ABC News*. Last modified 9 January, 2012. Accessed 13 March, 2016. http://www. abc.net.au/news/2012-01-09/toowoomba-queensland-floods-one- year-on/3761292.

Cash, David. "The Paris Agreement: The First Local Environmental Pact." *The Conversation*, 8 January, 2016, accessed 9 January, 2016. https://theconversation.com/the-paris-agreement-the-first-local-global-environmental-pact-52483.

Christianity Today. "1525 The Anabaptist Movement Begins." *Christianity Today, Christian History*. Accessed 10 January, 2016. http://www.christianitytoday.com/ch/1990/issue28/2838.html.

Conway, Martin. "The Bitter Fruits of Alienation: Belgium's Struggle is the Problem of Our Age." *The Conversation*, 24 March, 2016. Accessed 24 March, 2016. http://theconversation.com/the-bitter-fruits-of-alienation-belgiums-struggle-is-the-problem-of-our-age-56758.

Doherty, Ben. "Let them stay: Backlask in Australia against plans to send asylum seekers to detention camps." *The Guardian*, 10 February, 2016. Accessed March 31, 2016. http://www.theguardian.com/australia-news/2016/feb/10/let-them-stay-australia-backlash-267-asylum-seekers-island-detention-camps.

Eckersley Richard. "The Denial Behind Youth Suicide." *Crikey*, September 14, 2012. Accessed 22 May, 2016. http://www.crikey.com.au/2012/09/14/the-denial-behind-youth-suicide/.

Georgatos, Gerry. "Australia's Aboriginal children – The World's Highest Suicide Rate." *The Stringer*, 3 August, 2013. Accessed 21 May, 2016. http://thestringer.com.au/australias-aboriginal-children-the-worlds-highest-suicide-rate/#.Uc0x1pXmpvc.

Hasham, Nicole. "Hospital refused to discharge asylum seeker toddler to prevent return to Naru." *Sydney Morning Herald*, 13 February, 2016. Accessed March 31 2016. http://www.smh.com.au/national/nauru-baby-being-kept-by-brisbane-hospital-20160212-gmt3dg.html.

King, Robert. "Death and Resurrection of an Urban Church." *Faith and Leadership.* Accessed November 2015. https://www. faithandleadership. com/death-and-resurrection-urban-church.

McCrindle Research. "Church Attendance in Australia." *The McCrindle Blog.* Last updated March 2013. Accessed 10 January, 2016. http:// blog.mccrindle.com.au/the-mccrindle-blog/church_attendance_in_ australia_infographic.

McEnery, Thornton. "World's 15 Biggest Landowners." *Business Insider Australia*, 19 March, 2016. Accessed March 24 2016. http:// www.businessinsider.com.au/worlds-biggest-landowners-2011- ´3?r=US&IR=T#3-pope-benedict-13.

Websites

ABS. "1370.0 Measure of Australia's Progress, 2010." *ABS Statistics.* Last updated 15 September, 2010. Accessed 21 May, 2016. http://www. abs.gov.au/ausstats/abs@.nsf/Lookup/by%20Subject/1370.0~2010~Ch apter~Suicide%20(4.5.4).

Biblevic. "Project 217: The Social Environment and Young People In Australia Today." *Biblevic Wordpress.* Last updated February, 2013. Accessed 20 November, 2015. http://biblevic.files.wordpress.com/2012/01/ project- 217-report1.pdf

Business Dictionary. "Discontinuous Change." *Business Dictionary.* Accessed 23 May, 2016. http://www.businessdictionary.com/definition/ discontinuous-change.html.

European Environment Agency. "Executive Summary." *European Environment Agency, Synthesis Report.* Accessed 9 January, 2016. http://www.eea. europa.eu/soer-2015/synthesis/report/0c-executivesummary.

IAP2. "Public Participation Spectrum." *IAP2 Resources.* Accessed 17 March, 2016. https://www.iap2.org.au/resources/public-participation- spectrum.

United Nations. "Adoption of the Paris Agreement." *United Nations, Framework Convention on Climate Change.* Last updated 12 December, 2015.

Accessed 9 January, 2016. http://unfccc.int/resource/docs/2015/cop21/eng/l09r01.pdf.

Welcome to Australia. "About." *Welcome to Australia.* Accessed 21 May, 2016. http://www.welcometoaustralia.org.au/about.

Talks and Lectures

Gates, Theaster. "How to Revive a Neighbourhood with Imagination, Beauty and Art." *TED.* March 2015. Accessed March 2016. https://www.ted.com/ talks/theaster_gates_how_to_revive_a_neighborhood_with_ imagination_ beauty_and_art?language=en.

Langmeade, Ross. "Conviction and Openness: Dialogue and Witness in a Multifaith world." Lecture presented as part of a subject, Contemporary Mission Theology: Contextualisation, Dialogue and Transformation, 9 April, 2008.

Robinson, Ken. "Changing Education Paradigms," *Youtube, RSA Animate.* last updated 14 October, 2010, accessed 15 November, 2015. http://www. youtube.com/watch?v=zDZFcDGpL4U

Trotter, Penelope. "Postmodernism and Art." Lecture, Australian Catholic University, Melbourne, Australia, 2014.

Lightning Source UK Ltd.
Milton Keynes UK
UKHW020623080419
340664UK00010B/1418/P

9 780995 381513